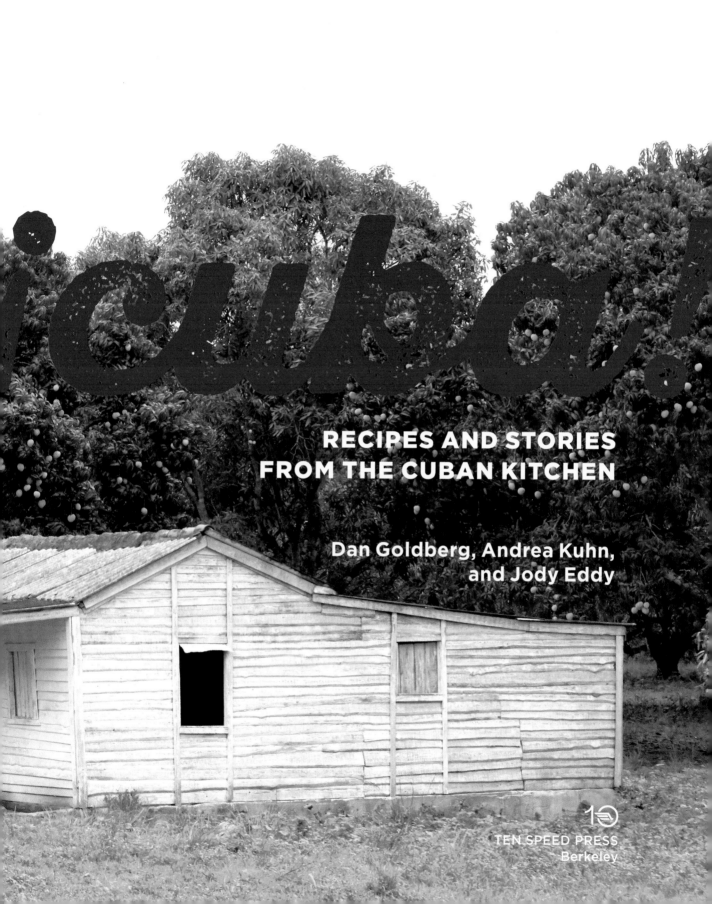

¡cuba!

RECIPES AND STORIES
FROM THE CUBAN KITCHEN

Dan Goldberg, Andrea Kuhn,
and Jody Eddy

TEN SPEED PRESS
Berkeley

introduction 1

1. basic training

2. snack & chat

3. pressed & starched

4. along the malecón

5. three amigos

introduction

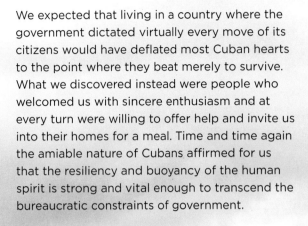

When we decided to journey to Cuba for the first time, we didn't know what to expect. It is a logistically challenging place to visit for most Americans, and we anticipated a slew of headaches leading up to our trip. We were pleasantly surprised that aside from a few travel hurdles such as obtaining visas and coordinating details ahead of our sojourn—official access to specific locations was subject to sudden change—getting to Cuba was not as overwhelming as we had expected.

What was even more remarkable, and much more gratifying, was the grace and extraordinary hospitality of the Cuban people.

We expected that living in a country where the government dictated virtually every move of its citizens would have deflated most Cuban hearts to the point where they beat merely to survive. What we discovered instead were people who welcomed us with sincere enthusiasm and at every turn were willing to offer help and invite us into their homes for a meal. Time and time again the amiable nature of Cubans affirmed for us that the resiliency and buoyancy of the human spirit is strong and vital enough to transcend the bureaucratic constraints of government.

After our first trip we immediately started planning our next visit, because we couldn't get enough of the Cuban people and their remarkable culture. Their passion for the sustenance that nourishes the soul, and sometimes the stomach—like music, art, dance, and food (and drink!)—sated our own appetites in a way that we have rarely experienced before. There is plenty of stress and deprivation in Cuba, but it does not dictate the lives of most of its people. Every visit we made proved to be a lesson, an affirmation that the fellowship of other human beings and the comfort and gratification gleaned from supporting each other without question or ulterior motives are phenomenal examples of humanity at its best. We decided to turn our experiences and photographs into a book because we wanted to share with others this extraordinary place and the remarkable people who inhabit it.

Dan is a photographer, Andrea a prop stylist and art director, and Jody a writer; together we worked on this project for five years. We visited Cuba three times during our book-writing journey to document a place that we have grown to love so much and to meet with its people who inspire us time and again with their extraordinary spirits and infectious hospitality. We cowrote this book as a love letter to a place and its people.

Initially, we thought we would write about Cuba's *paladares*, or independently owned restaurants, which are sustained by the nation's thriving black market. We quickly realized that today's *paladares* are primarily places where tourists congregate, their prices out of bounds for the average Cuban, and that we would discover the real cooking in Cuban home kitchens.

We visited kitchens in Havana that were shared by several families—the matriarch cooking for the entire clan, the patriarch waiting until everyone else had been served before taking any food for himself. We cooked in kitchens with grandmothers who invited us in after no more than a hello and a smile. We cooked at farmhouses where the bounty of ingredients was staggering, their freshness and flavor sublime. We even cooked on the back of a train car in huge iron pots with a woman who fed everyone passing through her town.

One of the things that astounds us in Cuba is the way the country changes so rapidly, transforming itself time and again to the beat of modernization and its ever-evolving political climate. A prominent market that was there during one visit was gone the next; a restaurant that we had enjoyed during our previous trip was transformed into a storefront selling cigars and rum. What doesn't change in Cuba is the rich culture and enduring warmth of its people. Time and again we were embraced by strangers as long-lost friends and welcomed into homes to cook, listen to music, and, if we were really fortunate (which we often were), engage in a little salsa dancing lubricated by a little rum (OK, a lot) and a puff or two on a cigar between songs. Food is prepared and enjoyed for hours over conversations that begin in the early afternoon and last long into the night. Every time we returned home from Cuba we craved those languid meals, those endless conversations, and the laughter and kinship they inspired, and every time we returned to open arms from friends and strangers alike.

We ate well in Cuba, not because the restaurants were astounding, but because of the home cooking—made with simple ingredients and easy techniques by an inviting person who wanted nothing more than to show us how to cook a one-pot wonder low and slow throughout an afternoon, infused with laughter and an irresistible hospitality. The recipes in this book are interpretations of these cooking and dining experiences in Cuba, reworked once we arrived back home to make them more doable for the U.S. home cook. We strove to document a food culture that is as challenging and complex as it is pleasurable and straightforward. A turbulent history has written the chapters of Cuban culinary traditions; they are frequently infused with hardship, but more often than not, as is true of the Cuban people themselves, in the end there is usually a note of triumph that trumps the struggle. Cuban foodways tell the story of tenacity and innovation, of creativity flourishing in spite of, or perhaps because of, a lack of resources.

The kindness we experienced while cooking in Cuban homes was remarkable, expressed with a graciousness that is a lesson for home cooks everywhere. We learned so much during these cooking lessons, not only about the ingredients, techniques, and traditions integral to the Cuban culinary repertoire, but also about how a dish, even in its most humble incarnation, tastes sublime when flavored with a desire to connect with food that not only delights the palate but gratifies the spirit, too.

"Whenever the Cuban people are given something that the government relinquishes control of, they tell us it is worthless and nothing good will come from it. We never feel their words in our hearts, because what lives there is a truth that will never be relinquished in spite of all that we have endured." We heard this from a farmer named Adolfo, on a road trip to the Vinales Valley, as he reached up to pluck a mango from one of the trees bordering the

property. He inhaled the aroma of its taut yellow skin deeply, then continued, "If we are given the opportunity, we can make anything happen; we can transform an infertile field into paradise. The problem is that we are never given these chances; we are always under the spotlight and are told what to do by people who assume we can't think for ourselves.

"But things are changing." He opened a cage to pet one of the rabbits who provide fertilizer for his farm, and continued, "Little by little, our prospects are improving and things are loosening up. We have waited a long time, but what has happened in all those decades is that, day by day, the energy inside of us expanded and became more potent. It is time now in Cuba to unleash it, to show the world and our own government what we are capable of. But most importantly, it is time to show ourselves."

This book documents a journey to explore the food and people of a nation on the cusp of fundamental change. So many aspects of this nation—crumbling façades, weathered patina, and vintage cars—symbolize a country locked in time, frozen in an era when its people brimmed with optimism and a seemingly limitless enthusiasm, spearheaded by the belief that each day would be better than the last. These are the vestiges of yesterday, emblems of the boom years when Cuba's cities, villages, and farms percolated with industry, thriving in a gilded time of innovation and joie de vivre that showed no signs of ending. And then it did. Fidel Castro and the Revolution he advocated brought industry to a standstill and essentially cut the Cuban people off from access to the rest of the world, ushering in a waiting game that Cuba is still locked into today.

The Revolution was followed by a well-documented period of deprivation and stifled dreams. Cuba's politics have long polarized people, most notably in the United States, to which many Cubans have migrated in search of a better life.

Just a few years ago a trip to Cuba was virtually impossible for most Americans, who didn't want to risk arrest by traveling there. The Revolution and what followed have long been relegated to our history books and may seem irrelevant in the context of our modern world, but it is still painfully relevant to Cubans. Traveling to Cuba still poses a few challenges for the American, but what the visitor receives in exchange is well worth a few logistical headaches.

Cuba is alluring because of the generous spirit of its people, its rich and storied history, and its miles of white sand beaches bordering a lush interior of dense tropical forests. It has also been tantalizing to many precisely because it is forbidden—a nation only ninety miles from mainland America, yet so isolated that it might just as well be located on another planet entirely. The decades that passed since the Revolution have instilled in the Cuban people a sense of dependency born of destitution.

"It has never been easy to be Cuban," affirmed Reuben, whom we befriended during one of our Cuban adventures. A charming Havana native who always wore a fedora and a ready smile, he displayed a wisdom, insightfulness, and eloquence belying his thirty years. He has earned his acumen through decades of maintaining his resilient spirit and infectious optimism despite a government system that seemed bent on extinguishing it.

We not only explored Havana during our time in Cuba but also hit the road in one of those remarkably preserved vintage cars to visit the countryside and the coastline, to discover deeper aspects of its cuisine, its history, and its people. Reuben was with us during our trip to Vinales, and he shared his thoughts during an outdoor lunch on the breezy veranda overlooking Adolfo's farm, the iron-red *mogotes* (domelike hills) encircling the valley like a protective embrace. Reuben took a bite of a *tostone* (fried plaintain) stuffed with a tangy conch-and-lobster seviche and savored it before continuing. "We have always been dependent on someone. First it was the Spanish, then it was the Americans, and then it was Russia. When Russia deserted us, we were left to rely on our own government. And look where that got us!" He grinned before downing another *tostone*.

Reuben's easygoing nature was characteristic of so many of the Cubans that we met throughout our adventures. There is a sense that since the going is tough and the tough can't get going, because they are bound to an island that they're not allowed to leave, they might as well embrace whatever is good and positive in their lives.

"Cubans care only about their friends, family, and food," Reuben told us matter-of-factly. "We don't care about politics. If we did, we would never get out of bed in the morning. Our lives are difficult, but there is magic in them, too."

Though many facets of this nation's society require processing with a healthy dose of skepticism, one cannot help but embrace its proud and hospitable people, who have managed to trump their circumstances by fortifying their culture with an invincible strength and uncompromising character. Their robust compassion for each other and for visitors is infectious. They enthusiastically welcome strangers onto their stoops and porches to share a Bucanero—a local Cuban brew—and a conversation that can easily wile away an entire afternoon.

We embarked on our first journey to Cuba expecting to discover an economy in the midst of revitalization. While that is true in some sectors of society, we quickly realized that the nation still has a long way to go to recover from decades of oppression. Our abiding hope for the Cuban people is that their invincibility will usher in new era in Cuba's tumultuous history. One day soon, we hope, they will wake up to discover that after so many decades of waiting, so many years of operating in survival mode, they are at

long last independent. At last they will be able to seize all the opportunities so long denied to them and make all their deferred dreams a reality.

Such a day may still only shimmer enticingly in the future, but the politics are finally changing in Cuba. Its virtual isolation from the rest of the planet is being chipped away, one innovative, privately owned organic *finca* (plantation, farm) in the Vinales Valley at a time. Adolfo's *finca* represents not only the Cuba of today but also the Cuba of tomorrow, a Cuba of possibility and liberty.

After a long afternoon lingering at the *finca*, we were served the last course of our meal just as a cool wind from the valley blew over the table, bringing with it the aroma of the mint and maguey flourishing in Adolfo's fields. Reuben took a big bite of the tres leches cake, drizzled with raw cane sugar syrup and topped with rum-infused whipped cream, then pointed excitedly at a bird flying between treetops on the edge of the *finca*. "Look quickly, it's a tocoroco!" he said, his mouth still full. He swallowed, then continued, "It's our national bird for two reasons. One is because its red, white, and blue feathers represent our national flag. But there's a more important reason too. The tocoroco will die if it is held in captivity. It requires its freedom in order to live. That bird is Cuba. That bird is me."

basic training

A typical home meal usually includes simple ingredients that are universally beloved by Cubans. Rice and beans are mainstays that are gussied up with vegetables such as yuca (also known as cassava) and malanga, fruit such as mango and plantains, and proteins like chicken and pork. Flavor enhancers such as mojo sauce and sofrito and rich beef and chicken stocks provide a little pizzazz (more on all of these shortly). Baguettes or white rolls are another staple often served alongside a simple garnish plate of raw onions and tomatoes.

Havana's cuisine rarely deviates from an amalgamation of urban market basics, but there is much more variety waiting to be discovered in the countryside. Ingredients that were once staples of the indigenous diet—such as rabbit, guinea pig, and goat—are not necessarily common, but it's also not a surprise to find them on a rural table. Outliers such as snake, alligator, iguana, and crocodile also turn up, especially in Baracoa in the Guantanamo Province of eastern Cuba. Red mole, a flavorful tomato and ancho chile–based sauce laced with precious Cuban

chocolate, is another rare but welcome rural discovery since the government exports most of the cacao beans grown in Cuba and very little of it remains for the Cuban people to enjoy. It is in the countryside that tenuous links to Cuba's indigenous past exist in backyards where cooking is still primarily done over charcoal in the slow, leisurely way that busy residents of Havana rarely have time for today.

What doesn't change when traveling between Havana and Cuba's rural regions are the basic foods beloved by everyone.

Without ingredients like rice and beans and fried plantains, Cuban cuisine would lose its identity.

No Cuban meal is complete without black beans and rice, and many Cuban recipes such as ropa vieja, a shredded beef dish, are deepened by the slow development of sofrito, a combination of onions, garlic, tomatoes, and other aromatics, at the beginning of the cooking process.

Sofrito also finds its way into many of the velvety stocks forming the foundation of most Cuban stews and soups. Stocks made with animal bones that impart a silken texture are cooked low and slow, infusing the home with a tantalizing aroma promising good things to come. Another flavor enhancer in the Cuban pantry is mojo, a sauce typically composed of garlic and citrus juice that adds vibrancy to dishes like baked fish or fried plantains. Bijol (see page 243) is beloved in the Cuban culinary repertoire—a proprietary flavor and color enhancer as it endows a dish with a cheerful yellow hue. Bijol is especially favored in rice; it transforms a ho-hum bowl of white grains into something a little more festive and bright.

In a country whose people have been denied their right to exist as autonomous citizens by each new wave of colonizers and then by a native dictator, the basics that find their way to the Cuban table each day—the rice, beans, plantains, yuca, sofrito, mojo, and heady stocks and broths—are symbols of resiliency and courage. Most fundamentally, they are a link to the past that is cherished by Cuban people today. Each humble recipe transcends the sum of its parts, representing how a little creativity and patience can transform even the most elemental ingredients into something tantalizing and beautiful.

congri

Congri is more than the everyday black beans and rice; it represents the union of Spanish and African traditions that are omnipresent in this nation and integral to the Cuban identity.

We experienced one of the most vibrant displays of this cultural amalgamation on Callejon de Hamel. The artist Salvador Gonzalez Escalone has illuminated the walls of this undulating corridor with colorful murals and sculpture in a style the artist refers to as Afro-Cuban. In doing so, he has transformed a Havana neighborhood that was once considered a slum into a dynamic corridor of culture and music. We arrived when one of the daily rumba sessions was heating up into a pulsating display of music and dance. It was pure joy; a celebration of the meeting of two cultures and a display of Cubans' uncanny ability to transform a bereft environment into something extraordinary.

No dish better exemplifies this marriage of Cuban and African culture than congri. When we tried it in a café near Callejon de Hamel after our morning rumba session, the vibrancy of the street satisfied our palates and the music pulsed in our ears. Whenever we taste it again, it will remind us of the compassion, open-mindedness, and humanity of the Cuban people.

The basic incarnation of this recipe is called congri (page 11) in Cuba. This version is fancied up with plenty of bacon, onions, peppers, and aromatics that bring out the best qualities of its bean and rice dancing partners. One surefire way to announce that this is a Cuban dish through and through is to add some of the bean cooking liquid in the rice's final cooking stage instead of discarding it after the beans are drained. This cloaks the rice in a deep amethyst hue, crowning this humble staple with the regal embellishment it deserves, while each grain soaks up the flavor.

Our friend Reuben's mother, Ana, a soft-spoken woman with a shy but easy smile, told us with conviction, "Cuban food without rice is not food." She should know. Ana is one of the organizers of an annual food festival in Havana called Visual Gourmet, which explores the intersection of art and food. Though rice paddies do exist in Cuba and the nation used to rely solely on its indigenous varieties, locally grown rice is a rare find in the modern Cuban pantry. Today most rice is imported from Asia or Brazil. It is hoped that as Cubans begin to explore their culinary traditions once more, they will rediscover their indigenous rice varieties.

RICE AND BEANS

SERVES 6 TO 8

1 cup dried black beans

2 bay leaves

2 teaspoons salt

3 slices bacon, coarsely chopped

1 yellow onion, diced

1 green bell pepper, seeded and diced

3 cloves garlic, minced

½ teaspoon ground cumin

½ teaspoon dried oregano

1 cup long-grain white rice

1¾ cups Chicken Stock (page 16)

Place the beans in a large pot and cover with water by at least 3 inches. Refrigerate and let soak overnight.

Drain the beans and place in a large pot, adding fresh cold water to cover by about 1 inch. Add the bay leaves and place over high heat. Bring the beans to a boil and lower the heat and simmer until they are just tender. Add the salt and continue cooking for 15 minutes. Remove from the heat and set aside.

Sauté the bacon in a large saucepan over medium-low heat until the fat has rendered out and the bacon is crispy. Add the onion and pepper and sauté in the bacon fat until the vegetables soften, 8 to 10 minutes. Add the garlic, cumin, and oregano and cook for an additional 3 to 4 minutes. Add the rice and stir to coat with fat. Add the stock and bring to a boil. Lower the heat to a simmer, cover the pan, and cook until the liquid has been absorbed, 25 to 30 minutes.

Drain the beans, reserving ½ cup of the cooking liquid. Stir the beans into the rice and continue cooking until the rice is tender, 10 to 15 minutes. If you need more liquid to fully cook the rice, use the reserved bean cooking liquid. Adjust the seasoning to taste with salt, keeping in mind that the chicken stock and bacon both contain salt, so you might not need more.

Not only is the rice in this recipe cooked in chicken stock to infuse it with a luscious chicken soup kind of flavor, but it's also colored a golden yellow with the addition of Bijol or saffron, depending on preference. Bijol is often referred to as the poor man's saffron, since it is much less expensive than its pricey counterpart.

YELLOW RICE

SERVES 6 TO 8

¼ cup olive oil

1 yellow onion, diced

Pinch of salt

3 cloves garlic, minced

2 cups long-grain white rice

3½ cups Chicken Stock (page 16)

1 teaspoon Bijol, or a pinch of saffron, soaked in a little warm water

1 cup frozen peas (optional)

Heat the oil in a large saucepan over medium heat until shimmering. Add the onion and a healthy pinch of salt to help the onion release some liquid. Sauté until the onion softens, 7 to 10 minutes. You don't want to brown the onion, just soften it. Add the garlic and cook for 2 minutes, until it is fragrant.

Add the rice to the pot and continue sautéing for a few more minutes, until the rice starts to smell slightly toasty. Pour in the chicken stock and stir in the Bijol. Bring the mixture to a boil, then reduce the heat to low and cover tightly. Cook over low heat until the stock has been absorbed. Taste and adjust the seasoning with salt, if necessary.

Add the peas, if using, and replace the lid on the pot. Let sit for 5 minutes, allowing the steam from the rice to heat the peas through. Fluff with a fork before serving.

WHITE RICE

SERVES 6 TO 8

2 cups long-grain white rice

3½ cups water

1½ teaspoons salt

3 tablespoons canola or vegetable oil

Place the rice in a fine-mesh strainer and rinse thoroughly with cold water.

Transfer the rice to a large saucepan and add the water and salt, stirring to dissolve. Stir in the oil and bring to a boil. Let the rice boil for 5 minutes, then lower the heat to a bare simmer, cover the pot, and simmer until the water has been absorbed, 10 to 12 minutes.

Remove the pot from the heat and let stand, covered, for 10 minutes. Fluff with a fork before serving.

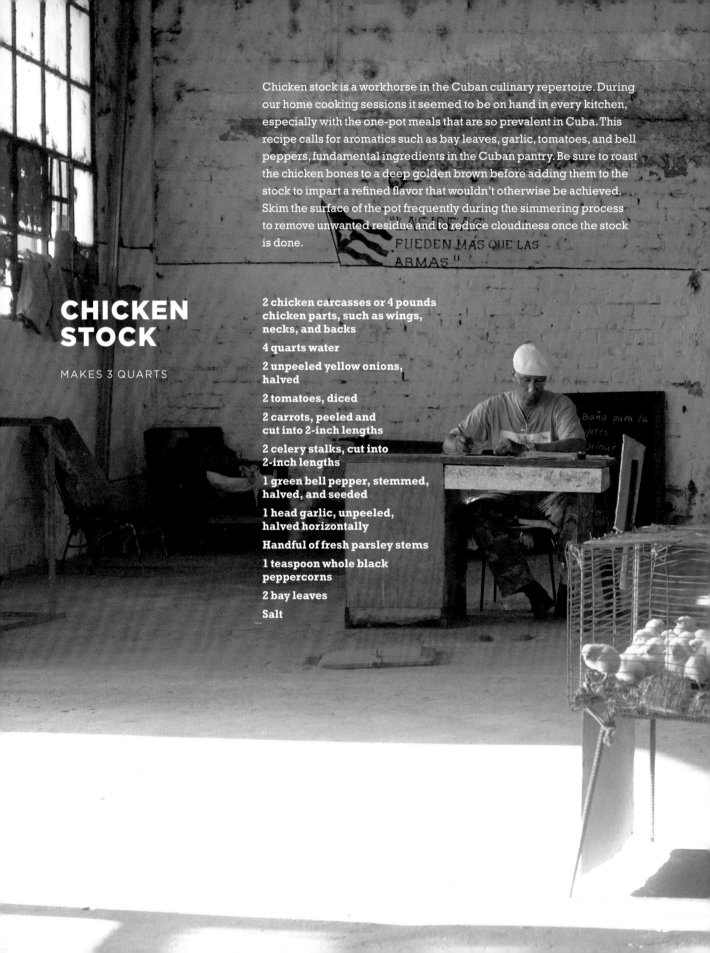

Chicken stock is a workhorse in the Cuban culinary repertoire. During our home cooking sessions it seemed to be on hand in every kitchen, especially with the one-pot meals that are so prevalent in Cuba. This recipe calls for aromatics such as bay leaves, garlic, tomatoes, and bell peppers, fundamental ingredients in the Cuban pantry. Be sure to roast the chicken bones to a deep golden brown before adding them to the stock to impart a refined flavor that wouldn't otherwise be achieved. Skim the surface of the pot frequently during the simmering process to remove unwanted residue and to reduce cloudiness once the stock is done.

CHICKEN STOCK

MAKES 3 QUARTS

2 chicken carcasses or 4 pounds chicken parts, such as wings, necks, and backs

4 quarts water

2 unpeeled yellow onions, halved

2 tomatoes, diced

2 carrots, peeled and cut into 2-inch lengths

2 celery stalks, cut into 2-inch lengths

1 green bell pepper, stemmed, halved, and seeded

1 head garlic, unpeeled, halved horizontally

Handful of fresh parsley stems

1 teaspoon whole black peppercorns

2 bay leaves

Salt

the water to a boil. Ladle a little hot liquid onto the baking sheet and use a wooden spoon to scrape up any browned bits, then pour it back into the pot. Lower the heat and allow the mixture to simmer for at least 6 hours and up to 12. Occasionally skim off the foam and scum that rises to the surface and discard it.

Remove the largest pieces of bone and vegetable with tongs and discard. Strain the stock through a fine-mesh sieve. Stir in salt to taste. Allow the stock to cool slightly, then refrigerate or freeze until needed.

Preheat the oven to 425°F. Place the chicken carcasses on a baking sheet and roast until golden brown.

Place the roasted bones, along with all of the remaining ingredients except the salt, in a large stockpot. Cover the pot and bring

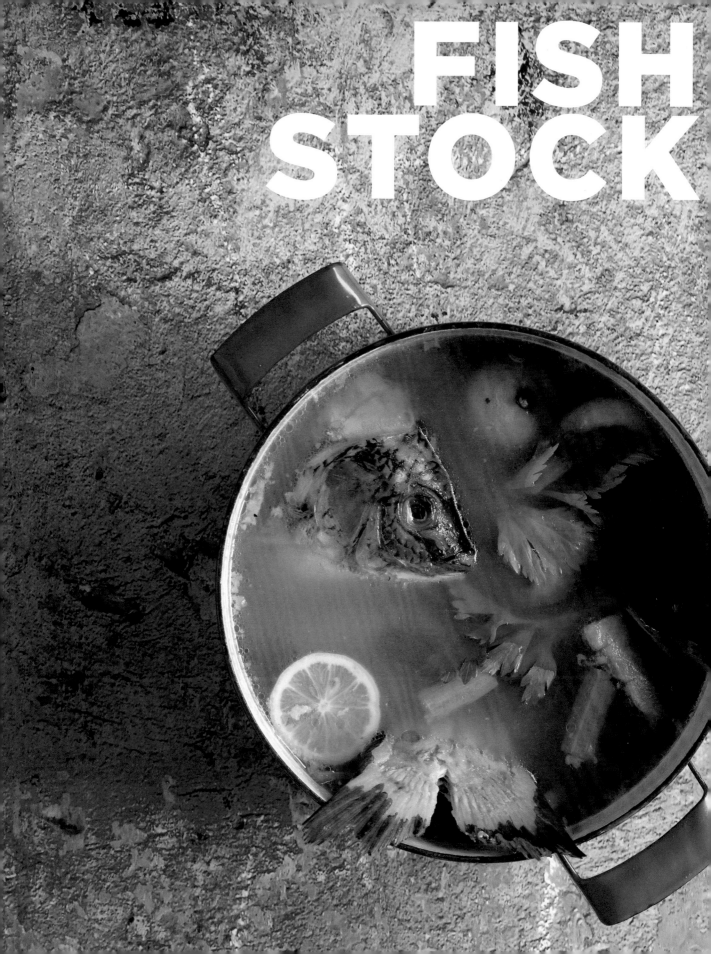

FISH STOCK

This recipe captures all of the aromatics that Cubans adore and delivers them wrapped up in the ocean, whose lapping waves have not only shaped the Cuban coastline but also defined the Cuban identity ever since the first settlers came ashore. The concept of making homemade fish stock sometimes sends even the most seasoned cooks running for their jar of bouillon cubes, but don't let it intimidate you. With a few hours of cooking and cooling time, along with fresh ingredients, you'll be well on your way to briny stock heaven. Be sure to rinse your fish parts thoroughly under cold running water before adding them to the pot.

FISH STOCK

MAKES 2 QUARTS

2 pounds fish parts, such as bones, trimmings, and heads, but no skin

10 cups water

2 tomatoes, diced

2 celery stalks, cut into 2-inch lengths

2 carrots, cut into 2-inch lengths

1 green bell pepper, stemmed, halved, and seeded

1 head garlic, unpeeled, halved horizontally

Handful of fresh parsley stems

1 tablespoon black peppercorns

2 bay leaves

Salt

Place all of the ingredients except the salt in a large stockpot and bring to a boil. Lower the heat to a gentle simmer and cook uncovered for about 45 minutes, occasionally skimming off any foam or scum that forms.

Strain the stock through a fine-mesh strainer and season it to taste with salt. Let cool and immediately use or refrigerate for 3 to 4 days. Freeze the stock if you need to keep it for a longer period.

Sofrito forms the foundation of many Cuban recipes. It's a simple combination of onions, garlic, and green peppers sautéed over very low heat. The only trick to making sofrito is to not rush, but to allow the ingredients to meld with each other slowly, much like a lazy sunset melting into the Malecón. The time required to coax out the flavor and enable this trinity of staples to transform into something altogether new pays off in big dividends for the palate. Make an extra-large batch and store it in an airtight container in the fridge for up to one week to add a little pizzazz to your next batch of beans, pot of rice, or pan of scrambled eggs.

SOFRITO

MAKES 1¼ TO 1½ CUPS

¼ cup olive oil
1 large yellow onion, diced
1 large green bell pepper, seeded and diced
Salt
4 cloves garlic, minced
2 tablespoons tomato paste
¼ cup white wine
½ teaspoon ground cumin
½ teaspoon dried oregano
Freshly ground pepper

Heat the olive oil in a large skillet over medium heat and add the onion and bell pepper. Add a pinch of salt to start building your seasoning. Sauté for 8 to 10 minutes, until the onion is translucent and the mixture is softened, but not browned. Add the garlic and cook for about 2 more minutes, until it is fragrant.

Lower the heat to a simmer, stir in the tomato paste, wine, cumin, and oregano, and sprinkle with salt and pepper. Simmer for about 10 minutes. Taste and adjust the seasoning, if necessary. Store the sofrito covered in the refrigerator or freeze it in small batches.

organoponicos

In recent years, privately owned, organic farms referred to as *organoponicos* have sprung up all over Cuba. These farms provide the creative ingredients that home cooks need to transform their basic recipes into something more interesting and refined. It is estimated that there are over seven thousand *organoponicos* throughout Cuba and at least two hundred in Havana alone. Urban farmers have increased from just under ten thousand in the early 1990s to well over forty-five thousand in the past decade.

Organoponicos were formed to fill the agricultural void created by Cuba's loss of Russia as a trading partner. By most accounts, the system is an unequivocal success. Not only do the *organoponicos* provide much-needed work for Cubans, but they also supply chefs and home cooks with ingredients that would otherwise be challenging to source in the city. The farms afford city-dwellers not only variety but also sustenance; it is estimated that they nourish over 90 percent of Havana's residents. Though *organoponicos* emerged in Cuba to fill a trade vacuum, their success in a city as busy as Havana has made them a template for urban farms all over the world.

During our first visit to Cuba we visited an enormous, thriving *organoponico* in central Havana. We lingered there for hours, meeting and sharing laughter with many of the female vendors. On our second trip, we visited again and were thrilled to be remembered and welcomed with an embrace by the same women. We were excited to visit a third time—and heartbroken to discover that the market had been shuttered. Things are so fleeting in Cuba, and this was one of the changes that really drove that point home for us.

When we visited Egido Market in downtown Havana, the variety of fruits and vegetables available was impressive. Bins overflowed with tamarind, pineapple, peaches, custard apples, cherimoya (a fruit indigenous to the Caribbean that Mark Twain cited as "the most delicious fruit known to man"), maguey, mango, yuca, bean sprouts, eggplants, spinach graced with bright purple flowers, oregano, limes, mint, onions, garlic, tomatoes, plantains, legumes, and coconut. Here was the panoply of farm bounty that delights the Cuban palate, and the vendors were happy to fill our baskets with all that we needed to infuse Cuban staples like rice, beans, and plantains with much-needed flavor, character, and color.

Plantains are one of the most common ingredients used throughout the Caribbean and South and Central America. The tradition of cooking plantains was brought to the Americas by the slaves from West Africa and is now a mainstay in the Cuban kitchen. There are countless varieties of the long, starchy root; one easy way to distinguish them is to divide them into savory plantains, which require cooking before consumption, and dessert plantains, which are peeled and eaten raw. We offer a cooking preparation for both types in this recipe; both deliver the healthful benefits of protein and vitamins C, B_6, and A, along with potassium and magnesium. The trick to achieving the best results when frying plantains is to not overcook them: remove them from the bubbling oil just when they start to turn brown, and not a moment later. Our friend Pepe told us that plantains grow so close to the sea in Cuba that you can taste the sea in them; no need for additional salt. If your plantains don't convey these ocean notes, go ahead and sprinkle on a little crunchy sea salt. If you're craving a sweet snack instead, substitute a pinch of brown sugar or drizzle of honey. They don't keep well and should be consumed piping hot from the pan.

FRIED PLANTAINS

SERVES 4 AS A SIDE

Vegetable oil for deep-frying

3 ripe plantains, peeled and cut into diagonal slices about 1 inch thick

Salt (optional)

Heat at least 4 inches of oil in a large, heavy pot until it reaches 375°F. Working in batches, fry the plantains until they are soft and golden brown, 4 to 5 minutes. Use a slotted spoon to transfer the plantains to paper towels to drain. Sprinkle with salt, if desired.

TAXI

Our friend Reuben told us matter-of-factly, "I don't like vegetables, but yuca isn't a vegetable; it's like candy to me." We're not going to tell Reuben that this high-fiber tuber is in fact a nutritional powerhouse in the vegetable family. Yuca is high in phytonutrients, which are thought to provide anti-inflammatory benefits. It's also packed with antioxidants and is thought to minimize pain associated with arthritis. In Cuba, it's as familiar as a side of potatoes on an Irish table; it is typically prepared simply drizzled in oil and sometimes sprinkled with fresh white farmer's cheese. In this recipe, they're prepared as fries, since they are high in starch and hold up well during the frying process. They're an unexpected alternative to standard-issue potato fries, imparting sweetness that pairs well with the acidity of ketchup or a bright and creamy lemon mayonnaise. Reuben's mother, Ana, told us that in eastern Cuba, where indigenous traditions are still found, yuca cookies and yuca dumplings stuffed with pork are uncommon but highly prized delicacies.

YUCA FRIES

SERVES 4 TO 6 AS A SIDE

4 medium to large yuca, peeled and cut into 3-inch-long chunks
Vegetable oil for deep-frying
Salt

Bring a large pot of salted water to a boil. Add the yuca and reduce the heat to medium. Cook until the yuca is very tender and easily pierced with a fork, 20 to 25 minutes.

Drain in a colander, then cut the yuca into sticks, aiming for about 3 by ½ by ½ inch. If your yuca is relatively narrow, wedges might be more practical and easier to cut; they will still fry just fine.

Heat at least 4 inches of oil in a large, heavy pot over medium-high heat. When the oil reaches 375°F, add the yuca sticks, being careful not to overcrowd the pan, as this will cause the temperature to drop. Working in batches if necessary, fry the yuca until it is golden brown.

Remove the yuca fries from the oil using a slotted spoon and transfer them to paper towels to drain. Sprinkle them with salt while hot and serve immediately.

FRIED GREEN PLANTAINS (TOSTONES)

SERVES 4 TO 6 AS A SIDE

Vegetable oil for frying

3 green plantains, peeled and cut into 1½-inch lengths

Salt

Heat at least 4 inches of oil in a large, heavy pot to 325°F. Working in batches, fry the plantain slices for 5 to 6 minutes, until they are light golden and softened, but not browned. Remove the slices from the oil with a slotted spoon and set aside to cool slightly.

Increase the heat under the frying oil until it reaches 375°F.

When the plantain slices are just cool enough to handle, smash them flat; you can use the bottom of a mug or sturdy glass, or you can use a *tostonera* (plantain press) if you've got one. Make sure you apply even pressure, smashing straight down.

Return the plantains to the hot oil and fry until they are crispy, 3 to 5 minutes. Transfer the tostones to paper towels to drain. Sprinkle them with salt while hot and serve immediately.

Mojo is one of the primary flavoring ingredients in Cuba. At its most basic it's composed of garlic, citrus juice, oregano, and oil. Bottled sour orange juice is common throughout the Caribbean, but if you have trouble sourcing it, regular orange juice with added lime juice is a good substitute. Sunflower oil is the most common fat in Cuba, aside from lard and butter, but in this recipe we're using olive oil to further enhance the flavor of mojo-dressed recipes such as baked fish, fried plantains, and grilled chicken.

MOJO

MAKES ABOUT ¾ CUP

12 cloves garlic, peeled
1 teaspoon salt
½ teaspoon cumin seeds
½ teaspoon dried oregano
½ cup bottled sour orange juice, or ⅓ cup freshly squeezed orange juice mixed with 3 tablespoons freshly squeezed lime juice
¼ cup extra-virgin olive oil

Crush the garlic, salt, and spices into a paste using a mortar and pestle. Alternatively, add the garlic cloves one at a time to a food processor with the motor running. Stop the processor and add the salt and spices, then pulse to combine. Add the juice and mix well.

Pour the mixture into a small heatproof bowl or measuring cup. Heat the oil in a small pan over medium heat until nearly smoking. Carefully pour the hot oil into the garlic mixture (it may hiss and spatter) and stir to combine. Let the sauce cool and transfer it to an airtight container. It will keep in the refrigerator for 3 to 4 days.

snack & chat

Our friend Pepe told us about the time his mother accidentally dropped her beloved radio from her third-floor balcony. The radio shattered into pieces, but by the time she reached the bottom of her stairs to gather up the shards of plastic and busted wires, she had a solution to her problem. She replaced the broken plastic parts with cardboard and enlisted the assistance of her neighbor, a whiz at electronics, to piece together the rest. By the end of the day, her radio was in full working order again, its cardboard frame holding together the components of a radio that had seen better days but still delivered the same sound it had before—and in Cuba, that's all that matters.

We discovered throughout our travels that a Cuban will never question you if you are in need, and if they do not have an immediate solution for whatever ails you, they will find it for you without judgment. They support each other in this same way, creating for themselves an impregnable safety net that will always catch whoever is about to tumble off the precipice. There is a resourcefulness and inventiveness about the Cuban people, born of a struggle that ultimately resulted in a creative and unconventional approach to solving life's most challenging problems.

One way that Cubans fortify their familial and neighborly ties and solve their problems collectively is to pull up a chair on the porch and chat. These convivial sessions often stretch late into the evening. Kids are always a part of the fun, and since computers and their ilk are out of reach for many Cubans, games that would be considered throwbacks in America, such as marbles or baseball with a stick, are popular pastimes for the younger generations.

One of our grandmothers used to reminisce about a time in America when things were simpler, and because of it, people spent more time together, extended families enjoyed more meals with each other, and neighbors talked more frequently. It's still like that in Cuba, and we have much to learn from them, in our breakneck-speed world where we are more interested in staring at a computer screen during lunch than genuinely listening to a story the person across from us has to share or a sliver of wisdom they have to impart.

We know that this front-porch arrangement in Cuba is partially due to its citizens' lack of resources, but when we were invited onto a veranda one evening just as the sun was settling into a hazy pink glow, we knew instantly this would be one of the most enjoyable experiences of the trip. We felt privileged to join the conversation of a group of cordial strangers as they passed around a plate of chicken and poblano empanadas and a pitcher of mojitos.

Snacking, chatting, and helping each other out is what it's all about in Cuba.

There's more richness in this sort of kinship than could ever be found in the social media vortex that has vanquished this kind of quality time in the United States: together on the porch, a Cuba Libre in one hand and a conch-and-lobster-stuffed tostone in the other.

paladares

Cuba is a land where one can too easily die of privation, but it's also a land where one can live and thrive. This is the essential message of the Cuban movie *Strawberry and Chocolate* (*Fresa y Chocolate*), filmed in the building that houses Havana's most famous paladar, La Guarida. Paladares are the Cuban response to strict government rationing and somber nationalized restaurants that stifle creativity and fatigue the palate with their monotony.

Paladares used to exist only in the tiny dining rooms of home cooks who prepared meals composed of ingredients procured on Cuba's impressive black market. The results were far more tantalizing than anything available in the restaurants strictly monitored by governmental watchdogs. *Paladares* were not only a way to keep traditional recipes alive but also a source of revenue for the entrepreneurial home cooks who opened their doors to adventurous eaters.

The driver on one of our trips to Cuba, Roberto, was a virile man with a flirtatious eye and biceps the size of basketballs, who seemed to know every Cuban woman who walked by his car window. Roberto told us when we visited La Guarida, "Cubans want to work; we just need the opportunity." *Paladares*

provide that chance for many Cubans who have grown weary of their rations and empty bank accounts. Today, *paladares* exist legally as private restaurants; government officials still check up on them periodically but generally turn a blind eye, because they too desire black market delicacies like lobster and a cigar to conclude the meal. Most likely, they are sitting at a paladar table enjoying the meal themselves.

Since many of the dishes served in *paladares* are made with black market ingredients like lobster, beef, and chocolate, chefs can be more creative in their kitchens. They also can preserve traditional dishes—like ropa vieja, rabbit with red mole sauce, and pork adobo—that might otherwise disappear in the wake of the rationing system. *Paladares* are much more mainstream in Cuba today than they were even a decade ago. In contemporary Cuba they are an accepted part of the mainstream dining culture. They are still the restaurants that serve the best food, but they are also quickly becoming nostalgic symbols of the measures the Cuban people took to preserve their culinary traditions and ensure that places existed where food represented more than survival.

FRIED PLANTAIN CHIPS (MARQUITAS) WITH MOJO

SERVES 3 OR 4 AS
A SNACK OR SIDE

Vegetable oil for deep-frying
4 green plantains, peeled
Salt
Mojo (page 30)

Heat at least 4 inches of oil in a large heavy pot over medium-high heat until it reaches 375°F.

Using a mandoline or a very sharp knife, slice the plantains lengthwise into slices ⅛ to ¹⁄₁₆ inch thick. Immediately drop the slices into the hot oil and fry for about 3 minutes, until golden brown.

Remove the plantains from the oil using a slotted spoon, and transfer them to paper towels to drain. Sprinkle the plantains with salt while they are still hot. Serve warm with mojo for dipping.

CRISPY
PORK

"The government exports so many of the ingredients that matter to Cubans, leaving very little in the hands of the people here in this country," said an elderly gentleman who ran an antique shop in Havana, as his albino Tibetan terrier ran in circles around his legs. He didn't want us to use his name, but he told us that as long as we kept it confidential, he wasn't afraid to tell us that he thinks "the government is worthless." The antiques in his shop—relics of the past, everything from tattered Cuban flags to antique watches and weathered baseball gloves—were piled to the ceiling in topsy-turvy towers. He ran his fingers through the black ringlets of his granddaughter, Rosario. She was sitting on a rocking chair in front of the establishment's only fan, the fairy princess of vintage-ville. "One of the only things they let us keep is pork, and what a relief that is. I can't imagine where we would be without pork."

We think many Cubans would agree. Pork is a celebrated ingredient in the Cuban kitchen, and this recipe glorifies and intensifies pork's flavor. These crispy, lusty porcine hunks are made all the more addictive when dipped into Mango Salsa enlivened with a hearty squeeze of lime. Keep in mind that this recipe calls for 2 pounds of trimmed pork shoulder, which means that, depending on the amount of fat and gristly bits on the shoulder, there could be a significant loss of volume once trimmed.

CRISPY PORK
WITH MANGO SALSA

SERVES 6 TO 8 AS A SNACK OR APPETIZER

6 cloves garlic, smashed
1 teaspoon dried oregano
1 teaspoon ground cumin
1½ teaspoons salt
⅓ cup freshly squeezed lime juice
2 pounds pork shoulder, trimmed and cut into 1½-inch chunks
Vegetable oil for deep-frying
Mango Salsa (see recipe)

Stir together the garlic, oregano, cumin, salt, and lime juice in a large mixing bowl. Add the pork and mix with your hands, making sure all the meat is coated in the marinade. Cover the pork and allow to marinate in the refrigerator for at least 2 hours.

Heat at least 4 inches of oil in a large, heavy pot over medium-high heat until it reaches 375°F. Remove the pork from the marinade and pat it dry using paper towels. Working in small batches, fry the pork until deep brown, crispy, and cooked through, 4 to 5 minutes. Be sure to allow the oil to come back up to temperature between batches. Transfer the fried pork to paper towels to drain. Sprinkle with a little salt while hot. Serve with Mango Salsa.

MANGO SALSA

MAKES ABOUT 3 CUPS

2 cups diced fresh mango

¼ cup diced red onion

½ cup diced cucumber

½ cup diced green bell pepper

½ habanero, stemmed, seeded, and minced

1 tablespoon honey

2 tablespoons freshly squeezed lime juice

½ cup chopped fresh cilantro

½ teaspoon salt

¼ teaspoon freshly ground pepper

Mix all ingredients and let rest at room temperature for at least 30 minutes to let the flavors combine.

Papas rellenas are stuffed potato croquettes that were introduced throughout many Caribbean and South and Latin American nations by their French colonizers. In Cuba they are typically stuffed with pork, but in this recipe a picadillo that packs just the right amount of heat adds an unexpected twist to the typical potato croquette. When prepared correctly, they should have a slightly crispy shell that easily gives way to a creamy center. The cream cheese helps achieve this velvety texture, while the garlic gussies up the potatoes in aromatic finery. Be sure to allow time for the assembled rellenas to thoroughly chill before frying. The picadillo recipe produces about 3 cups of filling, but the recipe requires only around 2 cups. Save the rest in a covered container in the fridge for up to 1 week.

PAPAS RELLENAS

SERVES 4 OR 5

2 pounds russet or
Idaho potatoes

8 ounces cream cheese

¼ cup (½ stick) butter

4 cloves garlic, minced

Salt and freshly ground pepper

3 large eggs

3 tablespoons water

2 cups unseasoned bread
crumbs or cracker meal

2 cups Picadillo (page 47)

Vegetable oil for deep-frying

Peel and quarter the potatoes. Bring a large pot of salted water to a boil and add the potatoes. Lower the heat to medium and allow the potatoes to cook until they are tender and easily pierced with a fork. Drain the potatoes and return them to the hot pan over low heat, shaking the pan for a few minutes until the potatoes are fully dry. Transfer the potatoes to a bowl and mash them with a potato masher until they are mostly smooth. Mix in the cream cheese, butter, and garlic, and then season the mixture to taste with salt and pepper. Let the mixture sit until it is cool enough to handle.

While the potatoes cool, beat together the eggs and water in a small bowl. Place the bread crumbs in a separate bowl.

Spoon about ⅓ cup of the mashed potatoes into your cupped hand and lightly flatten it into an oval.

Spoon about 2 tablespoons of picadillo into the center of the potato mixture. Bring the sides of the potato cup over to cover the mixture, smoothing any cracks with your fingers. Repeat this process with the remaining mashed potato mixture and picadillo.

Dip each rellena in the egg, shake off the excess, and then roll it in the bread crumbs. Refrigerate uncovered for at least 2 hours.

When you are ready to fry, heat at least 4 inches of oil in a large, heavy saucepan over medium-high heat until it reaches 375°F. Fry the rellenas until they are golden brown and heated through, 7 to 10 minutes. Remove them from the oil using a spider or slotted spoon and let them drain on paper towels, sprinkling them with salt while they are still hot. Serve immediately.

PICADILLO

MAKES ABOUT 3 CUPS

2 tablespoons olive oil

1 yellow onion, diced

½ green bell pepper, stemmed, seeded, and diced

4 cloves garlic, minced

1½ pounds ground beef

½ cup tomato sauce

½ cup white wine

Salt and freshly ground pepper

¼ cup raisins

2 teaspoons capers

¼ cup sliced pimiento-stuffed green olives

Heat the oil over medium heat until shimmering. Add the onion and pepper and sauté until just softened, 5 to 7 minutes. Add the garlic and cook until fragrant, about 2 minutes. Add the beef to the pan and stir, breaking up the big chunks. Cook until the beef is browned, 10 to 12 minutes. Add the tomato sauce and wine and season with salt and pepper. Mix well, cover, and simmer for about 25 minutes.

Stir in the raisins, capers, and olives. Taste and adjust the seasoning to taste with salt and pepper. Allow to cool slightly before using to fill the Papas Rellenas (page 44).

At a *finca* that we visited in Vinales (see page 5), we were served a chorizo paste that we couldn't help but slather on every square inch of bread at the table. It was removed from its casing and whipped until creamy and smooth; cilantro imparted a clean flavor, and there was barely a hint of chile. It is this lack of heat that differentiates Cuban chorizo from other varieties throughout Mexico, Spain, and Portugal. If you can't locate Cuban chorizo, the Spanish variety, with its smoked paprika kick, makes an ideal substitute in this recipe. Tortilla Española, perhaps the most famous of all Spanish tapas, is a favorite in Cuba too, where it is served in local cafes as a way to fortify Cuba's enduring ties to Spain.

TORTILLA ESPAÑOLA
WITH CHORIZO AND POTATOES

SERVES 8 TO 10

3 cups peeled and
½-inch-diced Yukon gold
potatoes (3 to 4 potatoes)

1 teaspoon salt

12 eggs

¼ cup heavy cream

¼ teaspoon freshly ground
pepper

¼ cup plus 2 teaspoons
vegetable oil, divided

1 yellow onion, diced

1 red bell pepper, stemmed,
seeded, and cut into strips

⅔ cup ¼-inch-diced Spanish-
style chorizo (one 3.5-ounce
package)

½ cup fresh or thawed
frozen peas

Bring a medium pot of salted water to a boil and add the diced potatoes. Cook until just barely tender, 7 to 8 minutes. Drain the potatoes and spread them on paper towels to dry completely. Sprinkle with salt.

Preheat the oven to 350°F. Break the eggs into a large bowl and whisk until well beaten. Whisk in the cream, salt, and pepper and set aside.

Heat the ¼ cup of vegetable oil in a large ovenproof skillet over high heat until shimmering and beginning to give off tiny wisps of smoke. Carefully add the potatoes. Fry without stirring until the potatoes are brown on the bottom, 6 to 7 minutes. Turn the potatoes with a spatula and allow the other sides to brown. Transfer the browned potatoes to a plate.

Add the remaining 2 teaspoons of oil to the same hot skillet. Add the onion, bell pepper, and chorizo and cook, stirring occasionally, until the peppers and onions have softened slightly, 7 to 8 minutes. Return the potatoes to the skillet and stir gently to combine. Lower the heat to medium-low and pour in the egg mixture. Stir to coat all of the vegetables with egg. Sprinkle the peas over the top and place the whole skillet in the oven. Bake until the tortilla is set in the center, 20 to 25 minutes. Check for doneness by inserting a toothpick into the center. It should come out clean.

Using a spatula, loosen the tortilla all the way around the edge, then quickly and confidently transfer it to a platter. Slice the tortilla into wedges and serve it warm or at room temperature.

CODFISH FRITTERS

Cod is a fundamental ingredient in Spanish cuisine, especially when salted and transformed into bacalao. Bacalao was quickly adopted by many Caribbean nations, including Cuba, because when properly preserved it does not require refrigeration. When preparing this recipe, it's essential to soak the bacalao for several hours and then rinse it thoroughly under cold running water to remove as much salt as possible before cooking. This recipe is paired with a hot sauce whose heat index can be tempered by swapping out the fiery habaneros for jalapeños or another milder chile. If you decide to go full throttle on the heat, be sure to open up your windows when processing them. These fritters are also addictive paired with Picadillo (page 47) or Mojo (page 30).

CODFISH FRITTERS

SERVES 6 AS AN APPETIZER

1 pound salt cod (bacalao)
½ cup all-purpose flour
1 teaspoon baking powder
4 eggs
¼ cup minced yellow onion
2 tablespoons chopped fresh cilantro
2 tablespoons chopped fresh parsley
2 tablespoons minced red bell pepper
¼ teaspoon salt
¼ teaspoon freshly ground pepper
Vegetable oil for deep-frying
Lime wedges
Hot Sauce (see recipe)

Place the cod in a large bowl and cover with cold water. Let soak for at least 8 hours, refrigerated, changing the water every 3 hours. The cod can soak for up to 24 hours; the longer it soaks, the less salty it will be. Drain the cod in a colander.

Place the soaked, drained cod in a large pot and cover with fresh water. Bring to a boil, then reduce the heat and allow it to simmer for 1 hour. Drain the cod again and break it into flakes with your fingers. Roughly chop the flaked cod and set it aside.

Whisk together the flour and baking powder. Add the eggs, onion, cilantro, parsley, bell pepper, salt, and pepper, stirring to combine. Stir in the cod and mix until well combined.

Heat the oil in a large, heavy pot over medium-high heat until it reaches 375°F. Working in small batches, drop tablespoonfuls of the fritter batter into the hot oil. Fry until the fritters are golden brown and cooked through, turning to fry all sides, 5 to 6 minutes total.

Transfer the fritters to paper towels using a slotted spoon, and let them drain. Break open a fritter to check the center for doneness. Serve with lime wedges and hot sauce.

HOT SAUCE

MAKES ABOUT 1½ CUPS

1 tablespoon vegetable
or canola oil

1 medium yellow onion,
coarsely chopped

1 red bell pepper, stemmed,
seeded, and coarsely chopped

3 habaneros, seeded and
coarsely chopped

3 cloves garlic, peeled

¼ teaspoon salt

½ cup white vinegar

½ cup water

2 tablespoons freshly squeezed
lime juice

Heat the oil in a medium saucepan
over medium-low heat and sauté
the onion and red bell pepper
until softened, 7 to 10 minutes.
Add the habaneros and garlic and
sauté for 5 minutes more. Season
with the salt and add the vinegar
and water. Cover, lower the heat,
and simmer until the mixture is
very soft.

Carefully transfer the mixture to
a blender and puree until smooth.
Let the sauce cool slightly, and
stir in the lime juice. Taste and
adjust the seasoning with salt.
If the consistency is thicker than
desired, add a little water to thin
it. Let cool, transfer to an airtight
container, and refrigerate until
needed. The sauce will keep in
the refrigerator for up to 2 weeks.

Tostones, or twice-fried plantains, are derived from the Spanish word *tostar* ("to toast"). It's an appropriate name for them, since they are fried once before being pressed in a *tostonera* and fried once more before they are either consumed with nothing but a little salt or stuffed with something sublime like this recipe's lobster and conch filling. Be sure to use green plantains for your tostones; they will hold together best.

TOSTONES STUFFED
WITH LOBSTER AND CONCH

SERVES 8 TO 10

FILLING

2 tablespoons olive oil

2 (7- to 8-ounce) lobster tails, meat removed and cut into bite-size pieces

1 pound conch meat, cleaned and cut into bite-size pieces

2 teaspoons minced garlic

3 teaspoons freshly squeezed lime juice

2 tablespoons freshly squeezed orange juice

Salt and freshly ground pepper

1 tablespoon cold unsalted butter

¼ cup chopped fresh cilantro

TOSTONES

Vegetable oil for deep-frying

6 green plantains, peeled and cut into 1½- to 2-inch lengths

Salt

Lemon wedges

To make the filling, heat the olive oil over medium-high heat until it begins to shimmer. Add the lobster and conch and sauté for 3 to 4 minutes. The meat will still be slightly undercooked. Stir in the garlic and cook for about 2 minutes, until the garlic is fragrant, but not browned. Add the juices and simmer for 5 to 8 minutes, until the liquid is reduced by one-quarter. Season to taste with salt and pepper. Remove the filling from the heat and stir in the butter and cilantro.

To make the tostones, heat at least 4 inches of oil in a large, heavy pot to 325°F. Working in batches, fry the plantain slices for 5 to 6 minutes, until they are light golden and softened, but not browned. Remove the slices from the oil with a slotted spoon and set aside to cool slightly.

Increase the heat under the frying oil and allow it to heat to 375°F. When the plantain slices are just cool enough to handle, smash them flat with a *tostonera* or the bottom of a mug or sturdy glass. Shape each flattened plantain into a little cup. Return the plantains to the hot oil until they are crispy, 3 to 5 minutes. Transfer the tostones to paper towels to drain. Season with salt.

Spoon some filling into each tostone and serve hot with lemon wedges on the side.

Tamales were the food of choice whenever the ancient Mayans celebrated a festival, and their role in Mexico, where they originated, and in Cuba—where they were introduced between 1920 and 1950, during a period of active cultural and culinary exchange between Mexico and Cuba—has changed very little throughout the following decades. The foundation of the tamale—ground corn, or *maize molido*—has always played an important role in Cuban cuisine. While the story is unsubstantiated, our friend Reuben told us that when the Spanish arrived in Cuba in the sixteenth century and told the Cubans they were looking for gold, the indigenous Cubans assured them it existed in their nation—and then they showed them corn. Corn is gold in many recipes in Cuba, the tamale most especially. In this recipe they are stuffed with chorizo and country-style pork ribs and paired with a smoky poblano sauce. This alluring combination might even convince you (unlike the single-minded Spanish that corn really is as valuable as gold.

FRESH CORN TAMALES
WITH POBLANO SAUCE

SERVES 8 TO 10

1 pound boneless country-style pork ribs, cut into small pieces

½ pound Spanish-style chorizo, cut into small dice

1 tablespoon vegetable oil, if needed

1 large yellow onion, diced

1 large green bell pepper, seeded and diced

1 jalapeño, stemmed, seeded, and minced

Salt

4 cloves garlic, minced

2 tablespoons tomato paste

½ cup white wine

7½ to 8 cups fresh corn kernels, cut from about 10 ears of corn

½ cup lard

1 cup Chicken Stock (page 16)

About 2 cups masa harina

Freshly ground pepper

8 ounces (1 package) corn husks

2 cups Poblano Sauce (page 58)

Place the cut-up pork ribs and chorizo in a large skillet over medium-low heat and cook, stirring occasionally, until the fat begins to render. Raise the heat to medium-high and cook until all the fat has rendered and the meat is beginning to brown. Pick out the meat and set aside, leaving the fat in the pan. If there is less than 1 tablespoon of fat, add 1 tablespoon of vegetable oil.

Add the onion, bell pepper, and jalapeño to the hot fat, along with a healthy pinch of salt. Cook, stirring occasionally, until the vegetables soften, 8 to 10 minutes. Stir in the garlic and cook until fragrant, about 2 more minutes. Stir in the tomato paste and wine and return the meat to the pan. Reduce the heat to a simmer and cook for 5 minutes. Set the meat mixture aside.

Working in batches, pour the corn kernels into a food processor and process for a few seconds at a time until you have a chunky corn mush. Add the lard to the last batch and mix all of the processed corn together.

Pour the corn mixture into a large saucepan and cook over medium-low heat, stirring, until the mixture begins to bubble. Stir in the chicken stock. Begin adding the masa harina, ½ cup at a time, mixing well after each addition. The goal is a thick paste that comes away from the sides of the pan. Continue adding masa harina until the mixture reaches this consistency, stirring vigorously between additions.

Stir the meat mixture into the corn mixture and season with salt and pepper, bearing in mind that it should taste slightly overseasoned at this stage, as steaming will dilute the seasoning. Let the mixture cool.

Soak the corn husks in hot water for a few minutes, then drain. You will use 3 husks per tamale. Lay out 2 husks on a work surface with the wide ends overlapping. Place a third husk in the middle, overlapping both outer husks. Spoon about ½ cup filling onto the center of the third husk and pat it into a rough oblong shape. Fold over the long sides of the wrapper first, then fold up the two short ends to make a packet. Tie the packet closed with 2 pieces of kitchen string, one at each end. Repeat with the remaining filling and husks.

Stand the tamales on end in an 8-quart pot. Add about 3 inches of water and bring to a boil. Lower the heat to medium, cover the pot, and let the tamales steam for 1 hour, adding more water as necessary. Remove the tamales from the pot and let them cool slightly before refrigerating. The tamales will be very loose when they are first cooked, but will firm up as they chill. Refrigerate the tamales overnight, then resteam briefly to warm them. If you are reheating only one or two, a microwave will work just fine. Serve the tamales with Poblano Sauce.

POBLANO SAUCE

MAKES ABOUT 2 CUPS

4 poblano peppers

2 tablespoons olive oil

1 medium yellow onion, diced

4 cloves garlic, coarsely chopped

½ cup white wine

Salt and freshly ground pepper

Char the poblanos over the open flame of a gas stove, turning often, until the skin is blackened all over. If you don't have a gas stove, you can either grill the peppers until the skin is completely charred or place them under a broiler set to high heat and cook to the same degree. Transfer them to a heatproof bowl and cover the bowl with plastic wrap. Allow the peppers to steam in the bowl for at least 20 minutes to loosen the skins.

Scrape the charred skin off the poblanos with your fingers, and remove the stems and seeds. This will take some time, so be patient.

If the seeds are sticking, you can briefly rinse each piece, but it's preferable to avoid rinsing if you can, because you will rinse away some of the delicious charred flavor.

Heat the oil in a large skillet over medium-high heat and sauté the onion until it is softened and browned, about 10 minutes. Add the garlic and cook, stirring, until fragrant, about 2 minutes. Add the white wine and roasted poblanos. Lower the heat, and simmer for 5 minutes.

Pour the mixture into a food processor and pulse until you have a slightly chunky sauce. Season to taste with salt and pepper.

pressed starches

The Cubano—Cuba's own take on the venerable ham and cheese sandwich—was most likely invented in America for tobacco workers who immigrated to Key West, Florida, from Cuba to work in the cigar factories that were established there following Cuba's War of Independence in the late nineteenth century. This is a controversial claim for Cubano lovers who wax nostalgic for a supposed twentieth-century Havana brimming with Cubano shops. But actually, the chewy, gooey delight that is a true Cubano was developed in southern Florida by Cuban immigrants, who concocted them as a hearty lunchtime meal to get them through a day of cigar rolling. And until aficionados exported it back to Havana—largely to satisfy tourists who had gotten hooked on this Florida specialty *in* Florida—the sandwich was not the beloved mainstay in Havana that it had become in Miami.

There are Cubanos to be found in contemporary Havana, but most of them are an uninspiring version of south Florida's Cubanos. They are served on an untoasted white baguette stuffed with lunchmeat and cheese. So there's nothing extraordinary about Havana's Cubanos—but some restaurants in the city are trying to make up for lost time. One of the notables is the Arte-Pub, a trendy, black-and-white-tiled café in Little Havana that also serves the Mariner sandwich, a strange concoction of tuna and cream cheese that locals can't seem to get enough of.

There is possibly no sandwich more representative of Cuba's deep and sometimes troublesome ties to America than the Cubano, perhaps because it was invented outside of Cuba, an outlier that symbolizes how many Cuban immigrants felt when they arrived on U.S. shores. With each bite, Cubans who emigrated are reminded of the place, culture, and loved ones they left behind seeking a better life in "La Yuma," a slang term for America that Cubans derived from the 1957 western *310 to Yuma* starring Glenn Ford and Van Heflin. The Cubano represents the life that Cubans who moved to the United States had to invent for themselves once they arrived. The movie was popular at the time of the Revolution, and for Cubans who

felt oppressed by the new dictatorial regime, it represented a nation that still embodied the ideals of bravery and independence.

The American restriction on travel to Cuba for so many decades made us wonder if Cubans still perceived the United States as the paradise they once did when it represented the ideals of *310 to Yuma*. Or had the years of separation eroded the affection they once felt? On our first morning in Havana, as we took our first sips of café con leche and savored bites of creamy potato croquettes and slices of fresh papaya on an already steaming hot spring morning, our bed-and-breakfast owner, Brian, cleared this right up for us. A man with a buoyant spirit who never let anything rile his calm nature, Brian explained this essential fact:

"Ask any Cuban what the problem is between our countries, and they will tell you it's government to government. It's not people to people . . ."

The message we have always wanted to send is that there is no problem between the Cuban people and the American people. There has always been sympathy and compassion between us, and we welcome the changes that are coming as our nations finally open up their doors to one another."

Brian took a deep sip of his coffee before continuing. "But with tourism increasing from America, one thing we do fear is that it will bring the trappings of your country with it. We do not need fast food or reality television shows. We need cultural enrichment, antibiotics, computers in the schools, better technology, and machinery that will put our people to work. We don't need what we perceive America to be. The new history between us needs to develop in an authentic way that enables the citizens of both nations to benefit from our improved relationship. If we take it slowly, we can ensure that we will both see the best in each other, and this will mean a positive union that we have all been waiting on for far too long."

The Cubano and its history and significance began in Miami—where it was the fuel that the immigrant Cuban cigar rollers relied on. Here it's served with a hearty stuffing of roast pork, sweet ham, and Swiss cheese. It's endlessly flexible, and any leftover pork from the lechon asado (page 115) would make a tasty filling.

THE CUBANO

SERVES 2, GENEROUSLY

1 loaf Cuban bread or a long loaf of Italian bread

Yellow mustard

½ pound sliced Swiss cheese

12 slices roast pork

12 slices sweet (not smoked) ham

2 dill pickles, thinly sliced

Unsalted butter

Slice the bread in half lengthwise, then again crosswise so you have bread for 2 large sandwiches. Spread both of the top and bottom halves with a thin layer of yellow mustard. Starting with the bottom halves, build the sandwiches, layering cheese, pork, ham, pickles, and a little more cheese, all topped with a mustard-spread lid.

Heat a griddle or cast-iron skillet over medium-low heat. Spread a little butter on the outside of the sandwiches and place them in the pan. Press down on the sandwiches with a sandwich press, a small cast-iron skillet, or a bacon press to flatten them. Cook for 7 to 8 minutes, then flip to brown the other side. Slice the sandwiches diagonally and serve hot.

This is not your standard-issue hamburger. It contains chorizo and a generous dose of Spanish paprika. If you don't have a sausage grinder to process the chorizo, ask your butcher to do it for you, or remove the casings and pass it through the grating blade of a food processor. Store-bought shoestring potatoes are the fixin' of choice in Cuba. They add an unexpected crunch to the burger and are complemented by tangy ketchup, creamy mayo, and a heaping spoonful of sweet pickle relish.

HAMBURGER
WITH CRISPY SHOESTRING POTATOES

SERVES 6 TO 12

2½ pounds ground beef

1 pound ground Spanish-style chorizo

3 cloves garlic, minced

2 teaspoons salt

1 tablespoon smoked paprika

1 teaspoon celery salt

1 teaspoon hot sauce

1 tablespoon plus 4 to 6 teaspoons vegetable oil

1 yellow onion, sliced into rings

Pinch of salt

½ cup ketchup

½ cup mayonnaise

3 tablespoons sweet pickle relish

12 hamburger buns

1 can shoestring potatoes

Mix the ground beef, chorizo, garlic, salt, paprika, celery salt, and hot sauce in a large bowl until well combined. Shape into 12 thin patties roughly 5 inches in diameter.

Heat 2 teaspoons of the vegetable oil in a large skillet over medium-high heat until shimmering. Add the patties in batches, making sure not to overcrowd the pan. Cook until the patties are crispy on one side (6 to 8 minutes), then flip to cook through. Wipe out the pan between batches and add fresh oil as necessary. Set the cooked patties aside.

Wipe out the pan once more and add 1 tablespoon vegetable oil. Add the onion and salt. Sauté until the onion is slightly browned and soft, about 10 minutes.

Stir together the ketchup, mayonnaise, and relish in a small bowl.

Slice the hamburger buns in half and spread both the top and bottom halves with sauce. Place a patty on each bottom half and top with sautéed onion and shoestring potatoes. Finish with the top buns and serve immediately.

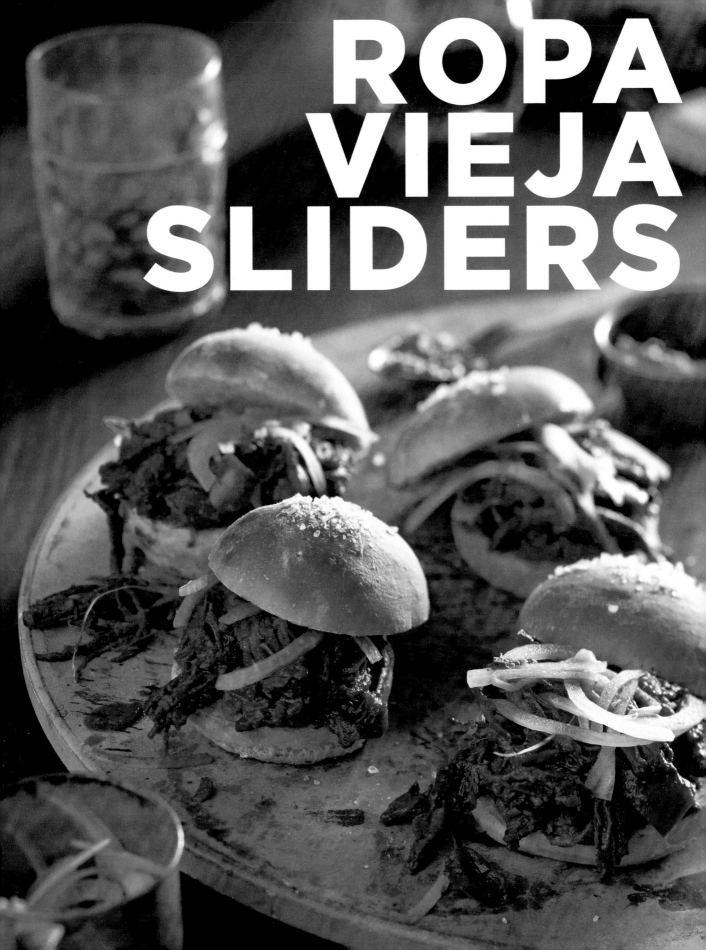

ROPA VIEJA SLIDERS

Ropa vieja is Spanish for "old clothes." It came to Cuba by way of Spain, which adopted it from the original Sephardic recipe, and it has become so adored by Cubans that it has been deemed the national dish. One bite of this slowly simmered shredded beef, amplified with tomatoes, garlic, cumin, paprika, and cilantro, and it's easy to see why. In this recipe, the traditional Cuban dish is served in a bun with a heaping pile of acidic pickled onions, a dish that makes a winning game-day snack or unique potluck contribution.

ROPA VIEJA SLIDERS

SERVES 5 OR 6

3 tablespoons vegetable oil, divided

3 pounds boneless beef chuck roast, cut into 2-inch cubes

1 tablespoon salt, plus more for sprinkling

1 large yellow onion, diced

1 green bell pepper, stemmed, seeded, and diced

8 cloves garlic, chopped

12 ounces light beer, such as pilsner or lager

1 ½ cups tomato sauce

2 tablespoons white vinegar

2 tablespoons tomato paste

1 tablespoon ground cumin

1 tablespoon paprika

1 teaspoon sugar

½ teaspoon freshly ground black pepper

3 tablespoons chopped fresh cilantro

12 slider buns, split

Pickled Onions (see recipe)

Heat 2 tablespoons of the oil in a large Dutch oven or heavy pot over medium-high heat. Pat the pieces of beef dry with paper towels and sprinkle them lightly with salt. Working in small batches, carefully add the pieces of beef to the oil and sear until well browned on all sides.

Add the remaining 1 tablespoon oil to the pot and then add the onion and pepper. Reduce the heat to medium and cook for 7 to 8 minutes, until slightly softened. Add the garlic and cook for 2 more minutes, until fragrant. Stir in the beer, tomato sauce, vinegar, tomato paste, cumin, paprika, sugar, 1 tablespoon salt, pepper, and cilantro. Return the beef to the pot and mix well. Cover the pot and simmer over very low heat for 2 to 2½ hours, until the meat is fork-tender. Use two forks to shred the meat in the sauce.

Stuff the slider buns with the warm *ropa vieja* and top with pickled onions.

PICKLED ONIONS

MAKES ABOUT ½ CUP

1 red onion, thinly sliced
1 cup white vinegar
¼ cup sugar
2 teaspoons salt
½ teaspoon whole black peppercorns

Place the onion in a nonreactive bowl. Heat the vinegar, sugar, salt, and peppercorns in a small saucepan until the sugar dissolves and the liquid just comes to a boil. Pour the hot liquid over the onions and let them sit, stirring occasionally, until cool.

rations

The years that followed the Cuban Revolution, which took place from 1953 to 1959, fundamentally transformed this island nation and profoundly altered its food culture. Before the Revolution, the American-backed President Fulgencio Batista, a former soldier, initially led as a progressive but eventually did away with elections and implemented a near-dictatorial rule. Before he was overthrown during the Revolution, Batista forged ties with organized crime and indulged the United States in its desire to gain more military and economic control in Cuba, ushering in a period of instability and high unemployment.

Fidel Castro's promise of progressive social reforms that would ensure equality for every citizen was initially greeted as a welcome change by the Cubans, who had grown weary of Batista's militarized regime. This perception quickly changed for many in the population, who realized shortly after the Revolution that the misguided alliances Castro had forged had locked Cuba into trade deals with other Soviet nations that propped up their own economies but for Cuba proved little more than smoke and mirrors.

Cubans endured the decades that followed with a stoic grace that enabled them to withstand a suppressive regime, even as the paint peeled from their walls and their cars became painful reminders of a time not so long ago when they had been free to communicate with the world, offer opinions without fear of retribution, and practice their preferred religion without the threat of persecution.

Castro was so enamored with Marxist ideology that when the Soviet Union began to usher in reforms under the leadership of Mikhail Gorbachev in the 1980s, transforming its economy from one dictated by socialist principles to a more liberal, free-market system, Castro refused to budge. This meant even greater misfortune for the Cuban people.

In the years prior to Gorbachev, Cuba's economy was fortified by a Soviet system that welcomed Cuba's natural resources, like sunflower oil and sugarcane, into its socialist network of imports and exports among other Soviet nations. This frequently forced the Soviet Union to pay a staggering price for Cuba's exports compared to their actual market value. Eventually, the funds hemorrhaged to essentially prop up Cuba's economy became too much for the Soviet financial system to bear.

Since Castro refused to abandon the extreme socialism he had forced on his nation, even as the Soviet Union underwent reform, the Soviet Union officially severed ties in 1990, leaving Cuba to fend for itself, with few trading partners willing to pay inflated prices for exports they could purchase more cheaply elsewhere.

This ushered in the "Special Period," an era from 1990 to 1998 that was special only in the starvation that Cubans suffered. The strict rations imposed on Cuban citizens included a monthly per-person limit of a few pounds of rice, beans, bananas (or potatoes), oil, flour, salt, and white and brown sugar, along with a daily ration of a small packet of coffee, one egg, and one bun, along with one cup of milk per day for children under the age of seven. Our friend Reuben shared his rationing story with us:

"I was seven years old when rationing began. My mom, dad, sister, and I each received one bun per day. I ate one bun in the morning, drizzled with a little oil and sprinkled with a pinch of salt, and was sent to school with a second bun prepared in the same way for my lunch. It wasn't until I was older that I realized that because I ate two buns per day, it meant that one of my parents gave me their bun and the other gave their bun to my sister, leaving them without even that small amount of food.

"My father worked for the Cuban government, and we were eventually sent to Zimbabwe for a few years during this time of hardship. The food seemed so plentiful in Africa, and once a week my parents would send to our extended family in Havana a shipment of food on a chartered plane. Sometimes I think it's the only reason we survived that dark and hungry time. Isn't it ironic that it was food from Africa, a continent known for famine and deprivation, that kept my own family from starving?"

Reuben's family lost more than food on their table during the 1990s. "My uncle was a psychologist who could not tolerate what was happening in Cuba when relations with the Soviet Union ended. He tried to flee to America twice and was caught each time and sent to Guantanamo Prison. The third time he tried to escape and the government apprehended him, they gave up and told him to leave and never come back to Cuba. He lives in Florida now, and although we talk to him on the phone every once in a while, we have not seen him since he left a few decades ago. It hurts my mother deeply."

Rations were not only brutal for the health of the Cuban people. Along with the nationalization of the country's restaurants, rationing also decimated their once dynamic culinary heritage. Food was eaten for survival during the Special Period; people had no time for creativity or the preservation of traditions. Havana's food customs were hardest hit, since rural people could still source some fruits and vegetables from the nationalized farms that the government strictly controlled.

This loss of culinary identity is still painfully obvious in many of the restaurants and home kitchens throughout Havana. Although there is more variety in the marketplace today than there has been for decades, the population is still in recovery mode.

JIBARITO

The *jibarito* originated in a Puerto Rican restaurant in Chicago when its owner read about a sandwich assembled with fried plantains instead of bread. This is our version of it, dreamed up while we were enjoying one in that restaurant. Our version uses chicken instead of steak, as chicken is much more affordable. If you prefer dark meat to white, substitute five boneless, skinless chicken thighs for the breasts. Either way, they'll be exalted with a heaping spoonful of the Green Olive Aioli included here.

JIBARITO
WITH BRAISED CHICKEN AND GREEN OLIVE AIOLI

SERVES 4

10 cloves garlic, peeled

½ teaspoon whole cumin seed

½ teaspoon dried oregano

1½ teaspoons salt

1 cup bottled sour orange juice, or ⅓ cup freshly squeezed orange juice mixed with 3 tablespoons freshly squeezed lime juice

3 boneless, skinless chicken breasts

2 tablespoons vegetable oil, plus more for deep-frying

Salt and freshly ground pepper

1 cup Chicken Stock (page 16)

4 green plantains, peeled and halved both lengthwise and crosswise

Green Olive Aioli (see recipe)

2 cups chopped iceberg lettuce or arugula

2 tomatoes, sliced

Drop the garlic, one clove at a time, into a food processor with the motor running. When all of the garlic is chopped, add the cumin, oregano, salt, and juice. Process until the mixture is foamy and well blended.

Place the chicken in a large zip-lock bag and pour the marinade over it. Refrigerate for 2 hours, turning occasionally to redistribute the marinade.

Preheat the oven to 300°F. Remove the chicken, reserving the marinade. Pat the chicken dry using paper towels. Heat the oil over high heat in a heavy-bottomed skillet, preferably cast iron. Sprinkle the chicken on both sides with salt and pepper. Carefully add the chicken to the pan using tongs. Brown one side, then flip and brown the second side. When the chicken is browned all over, pour in the reserved marinade and the stock. Cover the pan tightly with aluminum foil and place it in the oven. Let the chicken braise until it is fork-tender, about 1 hour.

Remove the chicken from the skillet and set it aside to cool slightly. Place the skillet containing the braising liquid over high heat and reduce it by about one-quarter.

Using two forks, pull apart the chicken into generous bite-size chunks. Add a few spoonfuls of the reduced braising liquid to the chicken and toss to coat. Taste and add salt if necessary. Set the chicken aside.

Heat at least 4 inches of oil in a large, heavy pot to 325°F. Add the plantain pieces to the hot oil and cook for 4 to 5 minutes, until the pieces float. Remove the plantains from the oil using a slotted spoon and transfer them to paper towels to drain. Increase the heat under the frying oil and allow the oil to heat to 375°F. When the plantains are just cool enough to handle, smash them flat with a heavy pan or by placing them between two cutting boards and pressing down. Return the plantains to the hot oil until they are crispy, about 5 minutes.

To assemble the sandwiches, spread Green Olive Aioli on a piece of plantain. Top with chicken chunks, lettuce, tomato, and another piece of plantain spread with the aioli. Repeat with the remaining ingredients. Serve warm.

GREEN OLIVE AIOLI

MAKES ABOUT 1 CUP

¼ teaspoon salt

1 clove garlic, minced

¾ cup mayonnaise

2 tablespoons freshly squeezed lemon juice

½ cup chopped green olives

Freshly ground pepper

Sprinkle the salt over the minced garlic on a cutting board and use the side of a knife to mash the salt into the garlic, making a paste. Stir the garlic paste into the mayonnaise, then add the lemon juice, green olives, and pepper to taste. Taste and add salt and lemon juice, if necessary.

The trick to these black bean burgers is to ensure they stay together during the frying process. This recipe yields a puree that is slightly dry but wet enough to maintain its structure as it cooks. If it looks too wet, add a few more beans until the combination holds together but is not too sticky, since this will result in a gloppy mess in the pan. The cornmeal coating provides additional assurance that your burgers will emerge in one piece. Other beans, such as azuki red, can be substituted for the black beans. The addition of Pineapple Avocado Salsa makes this recipe just right for a hot summer day, and perfectly paired with a pitcher of mojitos.

CARIBBEAN BLACK BEAN BURGER

SERVES 6

2½ cups cooked black beans, divided

½ red bell pepper, stemmed, seeded, and chopped

½ large yellow onion, chopped

2 cloves garlic, minced

2 tablespoons chopped fresh cilantro

1 teaspoon ground cumin

¾ teaspoon salt

1 egg white

¼ cup fine cornmeal

About 2 tablespoons water

1 tablespoon vegetable oil

6 soft hamburger buns

Pineapple Avocado Salsa (see recipe)

Combine 2 cups of the beans with the pepper, onion, garlic, cilantro, cumin, and salt in a large bowl. Puree the remaining ½ cup of beans with the egg white in a food processor. Mix the puree into the other ingredients, vigorously mashing it all together (it's very satisfying to use your hands for this step). Sprinkle the cornmeal over the black bean mixture and work it in. If it seems dry, add a little water, 1 tablespoon at a time.

Shape the mixture into 6 patties. Heat the oil in a large nonstick skillet until shimmering. Carefully add the patties. If you cannot fit all of the patties in the pan at once, work in batches. Cook the patties until they are browned and crusty on the bottom, 5 to 6 minutes. Flip and cook the other side.

Serve each patty on a hamburger bun, topped with Pineapple Avocado Salsa.

PINEAPPLE AVOCADO SALSA

MAKES ABOUT 3 CUPS

2 cups ½-inch diced fresh pineapple

1 avocado, cut into ½-inch dice

¼ cup ¼-inch diced red onion

¼ cup chopped fresh cilantro

1 clove garlic, minced

3 tablespoons freshly squeezed lime juice

1 teaspoon honey

Mix all of the ingredients together in a bowl. Season to taste with salt.

SQUID INK
MPANADAS

Empanadas, or hand pies, are everywhere on the streets of Havana, a beloved afternoon snack when something is needed to bridge the gap between lunch and dinner. This colorful version is destined to be a hit at any party for its unusual color alone, but when the flaky filling is opened to reveal a luxurious stuffing of lobster and crab meat, there's no doubt that this appetizer will receive well-deserved accolades. The tradition of using squid ink in Cuba comes from Spain, most notably in a black paella recipe. Here is it used to blacken the empanada dough before it is rolled out and stuffed.

SQUID INK EMPANADAS
WITH CHARRED RED PEPPER SAUCE

SERVES 6 OR 7

DOUGH

3 cups all-purpose flour

1 teaspoon salt

1 teaspoon sugar

1 teaspoon baking powder

½ cup (1 stick) unsalted butter, cut into cubes

¼ cup vegetable shortening

¼ cup white wine

4 teaspoons squid ink

2 eggs

FILLING

2 tablespoons olive oil

1 cup diced yellow onion

1 cup diced red bell pepper

3 cloves garlic, minced

2 tablespoons freshly squeezed lime juice

1 tablespoon butter

1 tablespoon chopped capers

1 pound cooked lobster meat, diced small

2 tablespoons chopped fresh parsley

2 tablespoons chopped fresh cilantro

Salt

1 egg

1 tablespoon water

Charred Red Pepper Sauce (see recipe)

To make the dough, combine the flour, salt, sugar, and baking powder in a food processor and pulse a few times to blend. Add the butter and shortening and pulse until all the fat has been cut into the flour and the mixture looks like clumpy sand.

Mix the white wine and squid ink in a small bowl, making sure the mixture is well blended. Beat the eggs into the squid ink mixture.

With the food processor running, pour the squid ink mixture into the dry mixture and allow to process until the dough comes together in a large ball. Turn the dough out onto a board and knead in any crumbly bits, making sure the dough is one smooth, homogenous mass. Flatten into a disk, wrap in plastic wrap, and refrigerate for at least 1 hour.

To make the filling, heat the oil in a large skillet over medium heat and add the onion and pepper. Sauté until the vegetables are softened, 8 to 10 minutes, then add the garlic and cook for 2 more minutes. Add the lime juice, butter, and capers, stirring to blend. Stir in the lobster, mixing thoroughly. The filling should be moist, but not soggy. If there is excess liquid, cook for a few more minutes over medium heat until it has evaporated. Remove the mixture from the heat, stir in the parsley and cilantro, and season to taste with salt. Set the filling aside to cool.

Beat the egg with the water in a small bowl and set aside. Remove the dough from the refrigerator. Working with one-quarter of the dough at a time, roll it out to about ¼ inch thick. Cut out 5-inch rounds by tracing the edge of a saucer or small bowl with a paring knife. Set aside the scraps from each batch of dough to combine and reroll at the end to get a few extra rounds.

Spoon about 2 tablespoons of filling onto a dough round. Use a pastry brush to lightly coat the edge of the dough round with the beaten egg mixture. Fold the dough round over into a half-moon shape and tightly seal, crimping the edge with a fork. Repeat with the remaining dough rounds and filling.

Line a baking sheet with parchment paper and place the finished empanadas on the baking sheet. Cover with plastic and refrigerate for at least 30 minutes.

Preheat the oven to 400°F. Bake the empanadas until the shells are firm, 30 to 35 minutes. Serve warm with Charred Red Pepper Sauce.

CHARRED RED PEPPER SAUCE

MAKES ABOUT 2 CUPS

2 red bell peppers
2 cloves garlic, peeled
1 teaspoon cumin seeds, toasted
1 teaspoon salt
½ cup mayonnaise
1 tablespoon freshly squeezed lime juice
¼ cup chopped fresh cilantro

If you have a gas stove, turn on a burner to high heat and place the peppers directly in the open flame. Roast until the skin is completely charred on one side, then carefully turn the peppers using tongs and char the other side.

If you don't have a gas stove, you can either grill the peppers until the skin is completely charred or place them under a broiler set to high heat and cook to the same degree.

Transfer the peppers to a bowl and cover tightly with plastic wrap. Let the peppers cool.

When the peppers are cool enough to handle, scrape off the blackened skin with your fingers. Pull apart the peppers, removing the stems and seeds, and place the strips of cleaned flesh in a food processor. Add the garlic, cumin seeds, and salt and process until nearly smooth.

Scrape the red pepper mixture into a bowl and add the mayonnaise, lime juice, and cilantro. Stir together and adjust the seasoning to taste with salt. Chill until ready to serve.

Lobster, especially the spiny lobster, is a black market favorite (see page 87) in Cuba, where it is consumed with a gusto reserved for life's rare luxuries. This lobster roll is a way to celebrate this beloved crustacean in a way that doesn't adulterate it too much, infusing its flesh with the flavor of the ocean. Add a little more mayonnaise if you prefer it creamy, and be sure to squeeze in a little fresh lime juice to add a summertime zing.

VEDADO LOBSTER ROLL

SERVES 4

2 live lobsters (about 1 ½ pounds each)

2 tablespoons mayonnaise

¼ cup chopped fresh cilantro

2 tablespoons chopped green onions, white and light green parts

¼ cup finely diced celery

2 tablespoons freshly squeezed lime juice

Salt

4 Cuban rolls, telera rolls, or other soft white sandwich rolls

4 tablespoons unsalted butter, softened

Bring a large pot of salted water to a rolling boil and add the lobsters. Cover the pot and cook for 8 to 12 minutes, until the lobsters are red and cooked through. The lobsters should cook for about 8 minutes per pound, so adjust the time up or down based on the size of your lobsters. (Because each lobster is cooking independently, base your cooking time on the size of each lobster, not their combined weight.) Use tongs to remove the lobsters from the pot and set them aside to cool.

Crack the shells using a lobster cracker or the back edge of a chef's knife and pick out the meat. Chop the meat into bite-size chunks. Place the lobster in a medium bowl and add the mayo, cilantro, green onions, celery, and lime juice. Taste and add salt to taste. Place the lobster mixture in the refrigerator to chill for at least 20 minutes.

Slice each roll in half lengthwise, stopping before slicing all the way through, so the rolls hinge open. Spread the cut surfaces with the butter. Heat a large skillet over medium heat and cook each roll, buttered side down, until browned and toasty. Stuff the rolls with the lobster mixture and serve immediately.

It was dusk the first time we strolled along the Malecón, a five-mile-long stretch of seawall with a grand esplanade that hints of better days. It was constructed in the early 1900s during a brief era of American military occupation. Today it's famed not for the role it played in protecting the city from the ocean waves that tend to swell on humid summer days, but for the young lovers who parade up and down the esplanade to the beat of car horns and their own yearning hearts.

This is where the vintage cars of Havana strut their stuff and where sometimes, if you're lucky, one of the fishermen who stand elbow-to-elbow along the quay each evening will invite you to salsa dance with them. This impromptu dance session ushered in our first taste of Havana's thriving night scene, and we could think of no better way to indulge than to be swept away in the arms of a fisherman, dancing to the tempo of a radio playing anemically somewhere in the twilight.

The smell of oil wafted off the bay into the sweltering night as the tempo increased beneath an inky sky spangled with stars. The astringent smell is a remnant of unregulated shipping, contaminants permeating the water from the ships that delivered cargo such as refined petroleum, machinery, medical supplies, and ingredients such as corn, soy, and wheat to the desperate nation in exchange for raw goods like sugarcane, tobacco, cacao, and coffee beans.

As we strolled along the Malecón one morning with our friend Reuben, he told us he had heard rumors that the Cuban government is working with a Japanese company to clean up the toxins. But he wouldn't believe it until the air blowing in from the bay smelled pure and the iridescent slick of oil along the surface of the water became nothing but a memory. Not believing anything until you see it (or in this case, smell it) is a familiar narrative in this nation where the fishermen refuse to let a little oil pollution detract from their salsa lessons.

along the malecón

Fishing, like nearly everything else in Cuba, is nationalized, which means that there is minimal profit for professional fishermen who play by the rules. But for the fishermen who line up along the seawall of the Malecón just as the sun fades to a hazy afterglow, there is the promise of hooking a fish to sell to a chef who trades in Havana's thriving black market, as nearly every chef tends to do.

Seafood has always been integral to the Cuban culinary repertoire, especially in towns like Trinidad, in the south-central portion of the nation.

Fishing villages are tucked into virtually every cove along Cuba's expansive coastline, and fish like marlin, jack, snapper, and the popular Cuban export spiny lobster appear on dining tables throughout the nation. We visited a black market fishing village on the outskirts of Havana where ramshackle fish huts of corrugated tin were used as mini processing centers for seafood

that would appear as the daily catch on *paladar* menus all over the city that evening.

Our friend Pepe, an older gentleman with a genteel spirit, eyes as blue as Havana's turquoise water, and gleaming silver hair, told us—as we ducked to avoid being smacked by the tail of a white marlin balanced on the shoulder of a passing fisherman—that the Hemingway International Fishing Competition had taken place a few weeks earlier. It was the first time that Americans competed—one more symbol of a tentative but steadily growing solidarity between the two nations.

Pepe nodded in greeting to a fisherman passing by with a cigar dangling from the corner of his mouth, carrying two needlefish by their tails. "It's time for us to meet once again after so much silence. We should be fishing together, working alongside each other, enjoying each other's company once more after all these long years of separation."

SHRIMP AND SCALLOP SEVICHE

This cooling summertime seviche is made with shrimp and scallops that would typically be accompanied in Cuba by mahi-mahi, one of the nation's most prized saltwater fish. The refreshing citrus combination of lime, lemon, and orange juices along with a flash of heat from the jalapeño and flavor hits from the cilantro, oregano, and red onion make this a prime summertime way to kick off a backyard barbecue. The crispy shredded plantains are enjoyable on their own, but when served alongside the seviche, they transform this into a little bowl of paradise.

SHRIMP AND SCALLOP SEVICHE
WITH SHREDDED PLANTAIN CHIPS

SERVES 6 TO 8

½ pound raw scallops, cleaned and cut into ½-inch dice

½ pound raw shrimp, cleaned and cut into ½-inch dice

1 small red onion, finely diced

1 jalapeño, stemmed, seeded, and finely diced

2 tomatoes, seeded and diced

2 tablespoons chopped fresh cilantro

2 teaspoons chopped fresh oregano

1 cup freshly squeezed lime juice

½ cup freshly squeezed lemon juice

½ cup freshly squeezed orange juice

1½ teaspoons salt

½ teaspoon freshly ground pepper

30 Shredded Plantain Chips (see recipe)

In a large, nonreactive bowl, mix the scallops, shrimp, red onion, jalapeño, tomatoes, cilantro, and oregano. Stir in the citrus juices, salt, and pepper. Cover with plastic wrap and refrigerate for 1½ hours. Serve with Shredded Plantain Chips.

SHREDDED PLANTAIN CHIPS

MAKES ABOUT 30 CHIPS

4 green plantains, peeled
2 cups vegetable oil
Salt

Shred the plantains using a box grater. Heat 1 inch of the oil in a large skillet over medium heat. Test the heated oil by adding a shred of plantain and making sure it starts to sizzle.

Carefully add tablespoonfuls of shredded plantain to the hot oil. Use a spatula to gently flatten each mound into a little patty. Cook until golden brown on the first side, about 2 minutes. Flip and cook on the other side. If the plantains are browning too quickly, lower the heat slightly.

Transfer the cooked plantain chips to paper towels using a slotted spoon and season with salt while hot.

Along the El Camino de las Especias (The Road of Spices) there's a contemporary spice shop showcasing seasonings from around the world. Cuban food is not known for its spiciness; the most popular aromatics are garlic, cumin, oregano, and bay leaves, with Sofrito (page 21) serving as the workhorse flavoring agent in the Cuban culinary lexicon. These langostinos pack a little more heat than would typically be found in Cuba; if you prefer to temper the heat, substitute red chile flakes or freshly chopped jalapeño for the habanero. A robust dose of lime juice enlivens the dish, and the freshly chopped parsley provides a garden-fresh finishing note.

CHILE AND GARLIC LANGO-STINOS

SERVES 4

6 tablespoons unsalted butter

8 cloves garlic, coarsely chopped

3 pounds whole fresh langostinos, cleaned, rinsed, and drained

6 tablespoons coarsely chopped fresh parsley

1 jalapeño, stemmed, seeded, and minced

½ habanero, stemmed, seeded, and minced

2 tablespoons freshly squeezed lime juice

Salt and freshly ground pepper

Melt the butter in a large skillet over medium-high heat. Add the garlic and sauté until fragrant, 1 to 2 minutes. Add the langostinos and toss with the garlic butter. Cook until no longer translucent, 7 to 8 minutes.

Add the parsley, chiles, and lime juice and stir to combine. Cook for 1 more minute to meld all the flavors. Season to taste with salt and pepper.

Sugarcane skewers imbue whatever they're holding together with a hint of the tropics. The skewers are available in many specialty Latin food markets, but wooden skewers work in a pinch. If you use wood, be sure to soak them for 20 minutes before use to avoid splinters. Be careful to prevent cross-contamination from the raw shrimp. Divide the glaze into two small bowls with separate brushes, and reserve one for the raw shrimp and one for the cooked.

GRILLED SHRIMP
WITH SUGARCANE

SERVES 8 AS AN APPETIZER
OR 4 AS A MAIN DISH

6 cloves garlic, minced

2 tablespoons freshly squeezed lime juice

2 tablespoons freshly squeezed orange juice

2 tablespoons dark rum

1 teaspoon salt

2 pounds jumbo or extra-jumbo shrimp, peeled and deveined, tails on

4 tablespoons butter

2 tablespoons dark brown sugar

2 tablespoons honey

1 teaspoon salt

2 cloves garlic, crushed

Mix the minced garlic, lime juice, orange juice, rum, and salt in a nonreactive baking dish or bowl. Add the shrimp and toss to coat with the marinade. Cover and refrigerate for 30 minutes.

While the shrimp are marinating, melt the butter in a small saucepan over medium-low heat. Add the sugar, honey, salt, and crushed garlic and stir until the sugar melts. Remove the pan from the heat and divide into two small bowls.

Prepare a medium-hot grill for direct-heat cooking. Remove the shrimp from the marinade and discard the marinade. Thread the shrimp onto 8 sugarcane skewers (about 2 or 3 shrimp per skewer, depending on the size of the shrimp), and brush them with one bowl of the butter glaze. If the glaze has solidified as it cooled, just reheat it slightly until it is liquid again.

Grill the shrimp skewers for about 4 minutes per side, brushing with the remaining bowl of glaze and a clean brush halfway through cooking, until slightly charred, sticky, and cooked through.

Discard any remaining glaze.

Jicama is a popular ingredient in Cuba, appreciated for its cooling properties and vibrant flavor. Here it's paired with grilled octopus and yuca fries for a dish that unequivocally evokes the steaming hot days of summer. As you're eating, pretend you're dining along the Malecón, watching the sun slip behind the waves gently rolling in to the Havana shore, and you'll transport yourself to Cuba with every mouthful. If you don't feel comfortable cleaning the octopus, ask your fishmonger to do it for you. Most likely its innards and beak will already have been removed; you should still be sure to rinse the octopus under cold running water and then pat dry with a paper towel before using.

GRILLED OCTOPUS
WITH JICAMA SLAW AND YUCA FRIES

SERVES 4 TO 6

1 (3-pound) raw octopus

1 lemon, halved

1 onion, peeled and quartered

2 bay leaves

1 tablespoon salt, plus more as needed

1 teaspoon whole peppercorns

2 tablespoons olive oil

Freshly ground pepper

Jicama Slaw (see recipe)

Yuca Fries (page 27)

To clean the octopus, make cuts into the body above and below the eyes to remove and then discard them. Remove the entrails and ink sac and discard them. Cut around the beak where the tentacles meet the body and separate them. Both the body and tentacles are edible.

Place the cleaned octopus, lemon, onion, bay leaves, salt, and peppercorns in a large pot and cover with water by about 3 inches. Bring to a boil, then reduce the heat and simmer for 45 minutes to 1 hour, until the octopus is tender enough to pierce with a knife.

Remove the octopus from the liquid and place it on a baking sheet. Set it aside to cool slightly, then refrigerate it until it is cool and firm.

Prepare the grill for direct, high-heat cooking. Cut the octopus into 2- to 3-tentacle segments. Place the octopus in a bowl and add the olive oil, turning to coat it evenly. Season generously with salt and pepper.

Grill the octopus as briefly as possible to get a good char without drying it out. Serve with Jicama Slaw and Yuca Fries.

JICAMA SLAW

SERVES 6

1 jicama, peeled and shredded

½ head napa cabbage, shredded

2 carrots, shredded

½ red onion, thinly sliced

⅓ cup fresh lime juice

3 tablespoons good olive oil

2 tablespoons sugar

Salt and freshly ground pepper

Toss all of the ingredients except the salt and pepper in a large bowl. Season the slaw to taste with salt and pepper and let it sit for at least 20 minutes to allow the flavors to marry.

The grill should be well heated before grilling the fish in this recipe, to prevent its skin from sticking to the grates. With a splash of Mojo (page 30) to enliven the crispy texture of the skin and the tender flesh beneath it, this quick and easy summertime meal requires little fuss but delivers plenty of citrusy flavor.

FISH
WITH MOJO

SERVES 4

2-3 (depending on size) whole yellowtail snapper or other whole fish such as tilapia or red snapper, scaled, gutted, and gilled

1 tablespoon vegetable oil

Salt and freshly ground pepper

Mojo (page 30)

Prepare a gas or charcoal grill for direct, high-heat grilling.

Make three diagonal slashes on each side of each fish to help it cook quickly and evenly. Rub both sides of the fish with vegetable oil and sprinkle with salt and pepper. Sprinkle a little salt inside the fish, too.

Bring the fish to the grill. Rub the grill with a rag dipped in oil and then lay the fish on the hot grill. Cook for about 5 minutes per side, until the skin begins to release from the grates and you can flip the fish without the skin tearing. Repeat on the second side. Transfer the cooked fish to a platter and serve with Mojo.

Just about every omnivore loves a good paella, and Cubans are no exception. It's the ideal dish for a large gathering, and there's nothing like the caramelized rice layer, called socarrat, on the bottom of the pan. This recipe is a celebration of the sea, source of many of Cuba's most valuable comestibles. If you don't have a dedicated paella pan, this dish is still entirely feasible using a large skillet that is at least 15 inches across and 2 inches deep. There are so many goodies in this recipe that this might make for a pretty crowded pan; if you find it's overflowing, you can also use a large, ovenproof baking container. This will unfortunately prevent the socarrat from forming, but you'll still have a nearly universal crowd-pleaser.

PAELLA

SERVES 8 TO 10

4 bone-in, skin-on chicken thighs

2 teaspoons salt, divided

2 tablespoons vegetable oil

1 pound Spanish-style chorizo, sliced into thin rounds

1 large yellow onion, diced

1 red bell pepper, stemmed, seeded, and diced

4 cloves garlic, minced

2 cups Valencia or other short-grain rice

1 teaspoon Bijol or saffron threads

1 teaspoon dried oregano

1 tablespoon smoked paprika

½ teaspoon crushed red pepper

¼ teaspoon freshly ground black pepper

2 cups white wine

3 cups Chicken Stock (page 16)

1 (14.5-ounce) can diced tomatoes, drained

1 pound raw large shrimp, peeled and deveined, tail on

3 tablespoons extra-virgin olive oil

1 pound mussels, washed and debearded

1 pound clams, washed

1 pound cleaned octopus (optional)

Lemon wedges, for garnish

2 tablespoons chopped parsley, for garnish

Preheat the oven to 350°F. Pat the chicken thighs dry with paper towels and season with salt. Heat the vegetable oil in a 15-inch ovenproof skillet over medium-high heat until shimmering. Carefully add the chicken to the pan, skin side down. Cook until the skin is golden brown and crispy, about 5 minutes. Flip and brown the other side. Transfer the chicken to a plate. Add the chorizo, onion, and pepper to the same pan and cook until the vegetables are softened, 8 to 10 minutes. Stir in the garlic and cook for 2 more minutes.

Add the rice, Bijol, oregano, paprika, crushed red pepper, 1 teaspoon of the salt, and the black pepper to the pan and mix to thoroughly combine. Stir in the wine, chicken stock, and tomatoes. Reduce the heat to low and cook for 20 minutes.

Toss the shrimp in a large bowl with the olive oil and the remaining 1 teaspoon salt. Arrange the shrimp, mussels, clams, and chicken thighs and octopus, if using, on top of the rice mixture, nestling them down into the wet rice a bit. Bake uncovered for 40 to 45 minutes, until the rice is tender and the chicken is fully cooked.

Serve with lemon wedges and garnish with parsley.

three amigos

Our driver, Roberto, was keen to show us his pig farm that he promised was just a few miles out of town. Roberto didn't speak a word of English, and when our friend Reuben wasn't translating, we communicated through head bobs and hand gestures. We didn't need Reuben's assistance to understand by the tone in Roberto's voice that his pigs were very important to him and it was impossible to say no, even though we had a packed schedule that day that we hadn't planned to interrupt with what turned into a twenty-mile ride from the center of Havana.

Along the way we passed by Lenin Park in the Arroyo Naranjo neighborhood. The park is a vestige of the late 1960s, dreamed up by a colleague of Fidel Castro, Celia Sanchez. She envisioned a 1,655-acre space where urban dwellers could gather for barbecues and recreation.

The park is the largest green space in the city and boasts an artificial lake, the Embalse Paso Sequito, along with a second lake resulting from the dammed Almendares River. Roberto reminisced about the afternoons in his childhood when his extended family would gather to grill pork, chicken, or beef between baseball sessions that lasted long into the night. As he told his story of Lenin Park, he seemed transported back to a time when urban spaces were cared for and resources were plentiful enough to prevent structures, such as Lenin's statue, from falling into disrepair.

Roberto's nostalgic tale—as translated by Reuben, who seemed to hit all of the sentimental inflections just right—told of a distant time when life was a little easier and held a bit more promise. This cast a heavy gloom on us until he pulled up next to a dilapidated apartment building and jumped out of his car, grinning enthusiastically.

"We're here," said Reuben. When he saw our confused expressions, he reassured us: "This is it; Roberto's farm. It's right over there beyond this building." He pointed to a ramshackle collection of corrugated tin doors and rusted iron bars.

Roberto opened a tin door and led us to a massive pig feeding a litter of fourteen day-old piglets. His pride was palpable, and we cooed over his newborns with as much gusto as we could muster. The farm boasted a few more pigs, several chickens, and four dogs that Roberto doted on after he finished feeding his pigs. He was so proud of his animals, and his work and his enthusiasm were infectious. Soon we were doting over the newborn piglets with equal devotion.

He explained on the long ride back to the city that he would sell his piglets on the black market once they were forty-five days old. They would find their way to the *paladar* tables we frequented and would fetch Roberto a hefty sum that would sustain him when his driving gigs waned. His farm would not measure up to most farms in America, but its value in Roberto's life seemed immeasurable. It provided him his livelihood, sustenance contained in the incessant squealing of fourteen day-old piglets born in the back of a tiny farm that formed the noble epicenter of our driver's life.

The value of meat in Cuba cannot be overstated.

It is not an everyday commodity for the average Cuban; chicken, beef, and pork are all held in high esteem, achieving star placement in many of this nation's most beloved recipes. Meat represents a level of luxury and abundance reserved for special occasions and honored guests.

During one of our trips we discovered that meat is prized not only for the revenue it generates for the producers but also for the fellowship it inspires. We were invited by our guide Amaurie to a pig roast taking place in the countryside about forty-five minutes outside of Havana. There we found that we were not only the guests of honor but also the butchers, when they handed us a Cristal beer and a hand-forged knife. Adrenaline surged until the pig appeared—and with it, our giddy energy was transformed into a sickened horror. We instantly knew that we would not be slaughtering anything on this trip, and we expected our hosts to be disappointed in us. But in true Cuban fashion, they were unfazed, slaughtered the pig themselves, and after hours of roasting it on a spit, served it to us and what seemed like the entire community. We all devoured it with reverence for the animal who gave its life for our meal. Salsa music pulsed, countless beers were consumed, and our porcine feast was buoyed by a festive atmosphere that only intensified as the hours ticked by.

Not a scrap of that pig was wasted; the leftovers were distributed among the farmer's friends and neighbors who stopped by to partake of the merry-making. We learned on subsequent trips, over and over again, that an abundance of precious chicken, beef, or pork almost always leads to a celebration culminating in a feast where everyone is invited to join in the fun, with the promise that they will leave having both sated their hunger and buoyed their spirits.

the santeria religion

Africa's influence is omnipresent in Cuba, with many of its citizens identifying as Afro-Cuban. Slaves were brought to Cuba from Africa to work in the sugarcane fields until the abolition of slavery on the island in 1886. At that point, African culinary influences—evident in ingredients like plantains and malanga and dishes like tostones and black beans and rice—had become fundamental to Cuba's culinary identity, and many of these recipes and ingredients also play a key part in the Santeria religion that many Afro-Cubans practice.

The Santeria religion, originating in West Africa, is a belief system of the Yoruba people who were brought to the island as slaves by the Spanish from the sixteenth to the nineteenth centuries. The Yoruba were referred to as the "Lucumi" by their Spanish despots, perhaps because the slaves referred to each other as *oluku mi*, meaning "my friend." Santeria is a derivative of the Spanish word *santos*, or a devotion of the saints.

It is estimated that nearly 80 percent of the country's citizens have ties to Santeria. Perhaps the religion's most profound influence on the foodways of Cuba

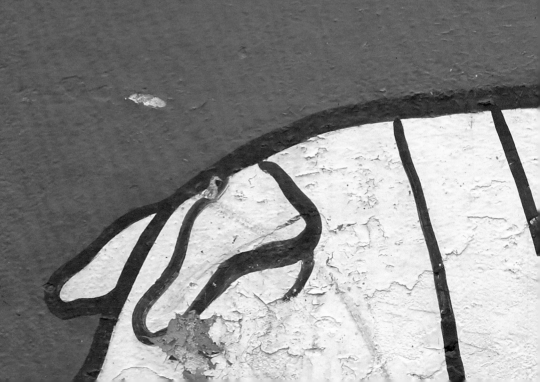

is its adherents' belief that food is divine and that the animal should be appreciated from conception to consumption. This mystical, humane approach to animal husbandry and butchery infuses Cuban meals with compassion.

On the last day of our final trip to Cuba, we tooled along one of Havana's side streets with Roberto and Reuben. We were late for our appointment with a black market flan maker, but despite this, Roberto slammed on the brakes when he saw a man carrying a basket of colorful statues on his back. He approached the car to enable Roberto to inspect his goods.

Reuben explained, "That's Chango, the Santeria god of thunder, war, and fire. It's Roberto's patron saint."

After days of hearing about the religion's gentler aspects, we were surprised to learn of its god, who symbolized conflict and natural disasters. Reuben quickly clarified, "Chango might oversee battles, but he is also the saint of dancing and music. He is a warrior." He paused. "But similar to many Cubans, he is a peacemaker, too." We understood it now; Chango represented the perplexing dichotomy that is Cuba.

SHREDDED
BEEF

This dish celebrates the simple wonder of a fried egg by placing it atop a bed of shredded beef and crispy yuca and drizzling it with mojo sauce. The beef and mojo can be prepared ahead of time, and the yuca can be boiled the day before. That leaves just reheating the beef, frying up the eggs and yuca, and assembling the dishes. It's well worth the effort for lunch or dinner or, as we prefer it, for breakfast.

SHREDDED BEEF WITH FRIED EGGS, MOJO, AND CRISPY YUCA

SERVES 8

About ¼ cup vegetable oil, divided

1 (3-pound) boneless beef chuck roast

Salt

1 large yellow onion, diced

6 cloves garlic, sliced paper-thin

1 (28-ounce) can diced tomatoes

2 bay leaves

Freshly ground pepper

3 to 4 cups water

8 eggs

Crispy Yuca (see recipe)

Mojo (page 30)

Chopped fresh parsley, for garnish

Heat 2 tablespoons of the oil in a large pot or Dutch oven over high heat until shimmering. Season the beef with salt and add it to the pot. Cook until well browned on one side, then turn and cook similarly on all other sides until the beef is browned all over. Each side should take 6 to 8 minutes.

Remove the beef from the pot and add the onion and a healthy pinch of salt. As the onion begins to release some liquid, use a wooden spoon to scrape up the browned bits at the bottom of the pot. When the onion has softened, about 8 minutes, add the garlic and cook for 2 more minutes. Stir in the tomatoes and

their juice and add the bay leaves, a little more salt, and a few cranks of pepper. Nestle the beef back into this mixture and add just enough water to nearly submerge it. Cover the pot and bring to a boil, then reduce the heat and simmer until the beef is falling-apart tender, 2 ½ to 3 hours.

Remove the beef from the braising liquid, allow it to cool slightly, and shred it. Transfer the beef to another pot and ladle in about 2 cups of the braising liquid and vegetables. Stir to combine and place over medium heat, stirring occasionally, until the beef absorbs some of the liquid, about 10 minutes.

For the eggs, heat 1 tablespoon of oil in a nonstick skillet over medium heat until shimmering. Crack an egg into the oil and sprinkle it with salt and pepper. Let the egg cook until it is partially set, then flip it over and cook very briefly so the yolk is still very runny. Repeat with the remaining eggs, adding additional oil to the pan if necessary.

To assemble, spoon about ½ cup of crispy yuca into a soup bowl. Top with the shredded beef, then a spoonful of mojo. Finish with a fried egg and an extra crank or two of black pepper. Garnish with chopped fresh parsley.

CRISPY YUCA

SERVES 8

3 medium to large yuca, peeled and diced into 1-inch cubes

Vegetable oil, for deep-frying

Salt and freshly ground pepper

Bring a large pot of salted water to a boil. Add the diced yuca and boil until tender, about 15 minutes. Drain the yuca completely.

Heat at least 4 inches of oil in a large pot over medium-high heat until it reaches 375°F. Working in batches, fry the yuca until it is golden brown, 7 to 8 minutes. Remove the yuca from the oil using a spider or slotted spoon and drain on paper towels. Sprinkle with salt and pepper. Be sure to allow the oil to come back up to temperature between batches of yuca.

Cubans love a good *lechon asado*, or grilled pork, not only for its flavor but also because it's enough of an enticement to gather neighbors, friends, and family from far and wide who revel in not only the goodness of the meal but also the convivial atmosphere it inspires. Mojo sauce is what makes *lechon asado* truly Cuban. The aromatics and citrus juice permeate the pork as it cooks, resulting in a dish that is as Cuban as the festive atmosphere it will inspire.

ROASTED PORK (LECHON ASADO)

SERVES 10 TO 12

12 cloves garlic, crushed

2 tablespoons salt

½ teaspoon dried oregano

½ teaspoon ground cumin

1 (8-pound) skin-on fresh ham or a pork shoulder or picnic ham with skin on

2 cups bottled sour orange juice, or 1¼ cups freshly squeezed orange juice mixed with ¾ cup freshly squeezed lime juice

¼ cup white wine

1 yellow onion, peeled and sliced into rings

2 tablespoons vegetable oil

Mojo (page 30)

Using the side of a knife, mash the crushed garlic, salt, oregano, and cumin together to make a paste. Cut tiny slits all over the cut face and underside of the ham with a sharp knife, leaving the skin side intact. Rub the paste into the ham, pushing some into the slits.

Combine the sour orange juice, wine, and sliced onion. Put the ham, skin side up, in a large pot or bowl that will fit in your refrigerator and pour the mixture around the ham. Cover the pot tightly and refrigerate overnight.

Preheat the oven to 275°F. Remove the ham from the pot and use paper towels to pat the skin completely dry. Rub the vegetable oil all over the skin. Place the ham in a roasting pan, skin side up, and pour the marinade around it. Tightly cover the roasting pan with aluminum foil, making sure the edges are sealed. Place in the oven for about 5 hours, until the meat is fork-tender, checking periodically to make sure there is still some liquid in the bottom of the pan. If all of the liquid has evaporated, add a little water to the bottom of the pan.

When the ham is tender, increase the oven temperature to 400°F and remove the foil from the roasting pan. Continue roasting until the skin is browned and crackly, about 1 hour.

Remove the ham from the oven and let stand for at least 30 minutes before slicing into it. Serve with mojo.

The origins of guava paste stretch back to Portugal, where quince paste was a popular pairing with cheese. When the Portuguese colonizers arrived in the Americas, they needed a substitute for quince, and guava had the same consistency and was close in flavor. It's enjoyed throughout the region as a filling for pastilles, as an accompaniment to cheese, and in this recipe as the foundation of a fruity barbecue sauce slathered on baby back pork ribs. Give your sauce time to lazily percolate to perfection before brushing it over your ribs. Cubans usually purchase their vinegar from the corner store, where it is dispensed from huge plastic jugs fitted with a spigot. The store owner fills up whatever container the customer brought, eyeballing its volume to calculate the cost. While you most likely won't source your apple cider vinegar in this recipe in the same way, when we make it we always recall those massive, ubiquitous jugs at the local mom-and-pop. The sauce stores well in a covered container in the refrigerator for up to a week and frozen for months.

RIBS WITH GUAVA BBQ SAUCE

SERVES 6 TO 8

2 (3- to 4-pound) racks baby back pork ribs

12 cloves garlic, peeled

2 teaspoons salt

1 ¼ cups bottled sour orange juice, or 1 cup freshly squeezed orange juice mixed with ¼ cup freshly squeezed lime juice

Guava BBQ Sauce (page 118)

Cut the ribs into 5- to 7-inch sections and place them in a nonreactive baking dish or bowl. Blend the garlic, salt, and juice in a blender or food processor until smooth. Pour the marinade over the ribs, cover, and refrigerate for at least 2 hours, turning the ribs occasionally.

Preheat the oven to 275°F. Remove the ribs from the marinade, reserving the marinade, and place them on a rimmed baking sheet lined with aluminum foil. Bake the ribs, uncovered, for about 2 hours, until the fat begins to render and the ribs are softened.

Remove the baking sheet from the oven and pour the reserved marinade over the ribs. Cover the baking sheet tightly with foil and return it to the oven. Bake for another 1 ½ to 2 hours, until the ribs are fully tender. You should be able to easily pull the meat away from the bone. Uncover the ribs and set aside to cool.

Preheat your grill to high heat. Brush the ribs with Guava BBQ Sauce (saving some for guests to slather on their portions) and cook for 7 to 8 minutes on each side, until the sauce is sticky and the ribs are slightly charred. Serve with the extra sauce.

GUAVA BBQ SAUCE

MAKES ABOUT 3 CUPS

1½ cups guava paste

½ cup apple cider vinegar

½ cup water

½ cup ketchup

1 teaspoon salt

2 teaspoons molasses

2 cloves garlic, minced

3 tablespoons dark brown sugar

2 teaspoons hot sauce, preferably habanero

Freshly ground pepper

Bring all of the ingredients except the pepper to a simmer in a small saucepan over medium-low heat. Cook for about 15 minutes, stirring occasionally. Season to taste with salt and pepper.

The preparation uses plenty of citrus juice and a generous helping of garlic cloves. Be sure to marinate your chicken for at least a few hours to intensify the flavor, and let it rest in its braising liquid to make it even more irresistible. It's the perfect dish for a cool autumn day.

BRAISED GARLIC CHICKEN WITH YELLOW RICE

SERVES 4

20 cloves garlic, peeled

2 cups bottled sour orange juice, or 1¼ cups freshly squeezed orange juice mixed with ¾ cup freshly squeezed lime juice

1 teaspoon dried oregano

1 teaspoon whole cumin seeds

1½ teaspoons salt, plus more as needed

½ teaspoon freshly ground pepper

1 whole chicken, cut into 8 pieces, or 12 bone-in chicken thighs

2 tablespoons vegetable oil

Yellow Rice (page 14)

Drop the garlic, one clove at a time, into a food processor with the motor running. When all of the garlic is finely chopped, turn off the food processor and add the juice, oregano, cumin seeds, salt, and pepper. Pulse a few times to blend.

Place all the chicken in a nonreactive baking dish or bowl and pour in the marinade. Cover and refrigerate for 2 to 4 hours, occasionally flipping the chicken and redistributing the marinade.

Remove the chicken and reserve the marinade. Pat the chicken dry with paper towels and season with salt.

Preheat the oven to 350°F. Heat the vegetable oil in a large skillet over medium heat. Working in batches so as not to overcrowd the pan, add the chicken, skin side down. Cook until the skin is deep brown and crispy. There's no need to flip the chicken and cook the second side; it will fully cook during the braising step.

When all of the chicken has been seared, either transfer it to a 9 by 13-inch baking dish or, if the skillet is ovenproof and large enough, return the chicken to the skillet. Pour the reserved marinade over the chicken, cover the vessel tightly with aluminum foil, and place it in the oven. Let the chicken braise for about 1 hour, checking it after 40 minutes. The chicken should be fork-tender.

Remove the chicken from the braising liquid. Pour the braising liquid into a saucepan and bring it to a boil for 6 to 8 minutes, until slightly reduced. Taste the liquid and adjust the seasoning with salt and pepper.

Turn on the broiler. Place the chicken pieces on a baking sheet, skin side up, and broil for a few minutes to recrisp the skin. Serve with Yellow Rice, spooning some of the reduced braising liquid on top.

Pork is not as precious as beef in Cuba, but it's just as revered. In this recipe, thick center-cut pork chops are marinated with grapefruit and brown sugar, which give it an exquisite sweet-and-sour finish. The citrus vinaigrette they're paired with finishes it off with the lingering note of a hot summer day, preferably by the beach on a Cuban shore.

PORK CHOPS
WITH WARM GRAPEFRUIT VINAIGRETTE

SERVES 4 TO 6

CHOPS
6 cloves garlic, smashed

1 tablespoon dark brown sugar

1 cup freshly squeezed grapefruit juice

2 teaspoons salt

8 center-cut pork chops

2 to 4 tablespoons vegetable oil

VINAIGRETTE
2 tablespoons vegetable oil

1 large onion, sliced into rings

Salt

½ cup freshly squeezed orange juice

½ cup freshly squeezed grapefruit juice

2 tablespoons white wine

2 tablespoons extra-virgin olive oil

Freshly ground pepper

3 tablespoons chopped fresh cilantro, for garnish

To make the chops, mix together the garlic, brown sugar, grapefruit juice, and salt in a bowl. Arrange the chops in a single layer in a glass baking dish and pour the marinade over them. Cover the dish with plastic wrap and refrigerate for at least 2 hours, turning halfway through.

Preheat the oven to 350°F. Remove the chops from the marinade and pat them dry with paper towels. Heat 2 tablespoons of the oil in a large, heavy, oven-proof skillet over high heat until shimmering. Working in batches, with additional oil if needed, so as not to crowd the pan, sear the chops on both sides, making sure to get a good, dark, crusty sear. If your skillet is large enough to hold all of the chops, return them to the skillet and place the skillet directly in the hot oven. If not, transfer the chops to a baking sheet and place the baking sheet in the oven. Bake the chops until they are fully cooked, 12 to 15 minutes. Test for doneness by inserting a paring knife into the thickest part of a chop and peeking inside. There should be no pink color visible.

To make the vinaigrette, heat the vegetable oil in a skillet over medium heat until shimmering. Add the onion and a healthy pinch of salt. Cook until the onions have softened and are lightly browned, 10 to 12 minutes. Add the orange juice, grapefruit juice, and wine. Lower the heat and simmer for 3 to 4 minutes. Stir in the olive oil, season the vinaigrette to taste with salt and pepper, and set aside.

When the chops are fully cooked, spoon the vinaigrette over the hot chops and sprinkle with cilantro.

pots & pans

We found out what formed the backbone of Cuban cuisine after an elderly woman on a third-story balcony called down to ask our guide, Amaurie, what he was doing with a team lugging around a conspicuous amount of camera equipment. He explained that we were working on a cookbook. That was all it took; she told us to come on up, and she tossed down her keys. We spent the afternoon cooking with her, kicking off the series of guerilla-style cooking lessons we experienced time and again in the home kitchens of Cuba.

In these humble kitchens we learned nearly everything we needed to know about Cuban one-pot dishes. Lessons like the critical importance of patiently layering flavors, giving each one enough time to reach its potential before adding the next. Once everything was assembled in the pot, we were taught to let it simmer slowly over a low flame, giving all the ingredients time to meld while adding their own special characteristics. Most importantly, we learned that even the most unassuming ingredients can be transformed into something extraordinary.

Beloved one-pot meals like black beans and rice, chicken soup, and goat stew are the backbone of the Cuban diet.

While many of them are an amalgamation of the different culinary traditions that influence Cuban cuisine, some of them, such as a simple but somehow unforgettable chickpea stew that we had at a restaurant called Los Nardos, are Spanish through and through.

We stepped into Los Nardos on the first day of our final trip, sweltering in the punishing temperatures of a typical spring morning in Havana. The restaurant is located up a steep flight of stairs in a dimly lit, cavernous, and, most important, ice-cold room buzzing with activity. The restaurant is funded by one of the many Spanish societies that support Cubans with ties to Galicia, Catalonia, and other regions in Spain.

After we had ordered—with George Michael's "I'm Never Gonna Dance Again" playing in the background—our friend Reuben explained that the Spanish connection is beneficial in more ways than one. It will assist those who can prove their hereditary affiliation to a particular region of Spain with financial support and even protect them from the governmental harassment common in Cuba. The rules are outlined in a doctrine referred to as "The Memory Law" that ensures at least a tenuous contract of allegiance and support for those who can prove their lineage. In essence, the societies promise these individuals certain financial, cultural, and social perks that form a safety net of sorts in a society bereft of them.

Chilled limeade and a pitcher of sangria, both house specialties, arrived as Reuben explained that the societies not only support individuals but also fund cultural endeavors such as choirs and art museums, along with community athletic teams that compete against each other for glory and the trophies that line the walls of each society's restaurant. In essence, societies fortify ancestral ties to Spain by forging relationships between members through cultural endeavors,

financial assistance, and assurance of a place to turn to in time of need. Nearly every one of Spain's geographic regions is represented by a society in Cuba; many own restaurants, but some are merely clubhouses where members gather for fellowship and support. Their brick-and-mortar locations are most prevalent in Havana, but they serve anyone throughout the nation who can claim an ancestral allegiance to the region they represent.

The omnipresent basics of black rice and beans along with fried plantains served on a wooden board arrived at the table along with a terracotta bowl of chickpea stew that evoked Spain's—and by tenuous default—Cuba's Moorish connection. A massive spiny lobster infused with hints of smoked paprika and anise soon followed, along with a plate of rock shrimp swimming in saffron sauce. The deliciously cold air in the restaurant, the refreshing limeade, and the sumptuous one-pot meal of chickpea stew revitalized us— along with the happy discovery of at least one established system ensuring many Cubans some measure of security.

Corn and chicken are both necessities in most Cuban pantries, and this recipe showcases both with elegant simplicity. The one surprise is the addition of pimiento-stuffed green olives. This dish is a prime example of how captivating even the most humble dish can be when given enough time to coax the very best from each ingredient.

CHICKEN STEW WITH CORN

SERVES 4 TO 6

CHICKEN

2 teaspoons salt

1 teaspoon smoked paprika

1 teaspoon ground cumin

½ teaspoon dried oregano

½ teaspoon freshly ground pepper

1 whole (3- to 4-pound) chicken, cut into 8 pieces

½ cup bottled sour orange juice, or ⅓ cup freshly squeezed orange juice mixed with 3 tablespoons freshly squeezed lime juice

2 tablespoons extra-virgin olive oil

8 cloves garlic, minced

STEW

2 to 4 tablespoons vegetable oil

1 large yellow onion, diced

1 green bell pepper, stemmed, seeded, and diced

2 cups Chicken Stock (page 16)

1 (15-ounce) can diced tomatoes

1 bay leaf

Salt

2 red-skin potatoes, cut into wedges

2 ears corn, cut into 1-inch-thick rounds

¼ cup pimiento-stuffed green olives

1 tablespoon capers

Freshly ground pepper

¼ cup chopped parsley

White Rice (page 14)

For the chicken, combine the salt, paprika, cumin, oregano, and pepper in a small bowl. Rub the spice mix all over the chicken pieces. Put the chicken in a large, nonreactive bowl and add the juice, the olive oil, and the garlic. Mix, making sure all the chicken is evenly coated. Cover the chicken and refrigerate, allowing it to marinate for at least 2 hours and up to 6.

To prepare the stew, remove the chicken from the marinade and discard the marinade. Pat the chicken dry, wiping off most of the garlic. Heat 2 tablespoons of the oil in a large pot over medium heat. Working in batches, brown the chicken, skin side down, until the skin is crispy. Flip each piece and brown the second side, adding more oil if the pot seems dry. Remove the chicken and set aside.

Using the same pot, add the onion and pepper, again adding more oil if needed, and cook them over medium heat until softened and beginning to brown. Return the chicken to the pot and add the stock, tomatoes, bay leaf, and a healthy pinch of salt. Bring the mixture to a boil, then reduce the heat and simmer for 30 minutes.

Add the potatoes, corn, olives, and capers. Simmer until the potatoes are cooked through and the chicken is fork-tender, about 30 more minutes.

Taste the stew and add salt and pepper to taste. Remove the pot from the heat and stir in the parsley. Serve over white rice.

Plantains are a classic Cuban ingredient that typically arrives at the table fried, alongside a plate of congri (see page 11). For this soup, they are pureed until silky smooth—and instantly refined and elevated. If you don't have access to plantains, parsnips would make a good substitute, since they have a similar starch content; either way, be sure to include the Crispy Shallots. They require some careful attention, but their delectable crunch enlivens even the most elemental soup recipe.

PUREED PLANTAIN SOUP WITH CRISPY SHALLOTS

SERVES 8 TO 10

1 tablespoon olive oil

1 yellow onion, coarsely chopped

3 cloves garlic, coarsely chopped

4 green plantains, peeled and cut into 2-inch chunks

2 quarts Chicken Stock (page 16)

2 tablespoons freshly squeezed lime juice

1 teaspoon ground cumin

Salt and freshly ground pepper

Crispy Shallots (see recipe)

Heat the oil in a large pot over medium heat. Add the onion and sauté until softened but not browned, 8 to 10 minutes. Add the garlic and sauté until fragrant, about 2 minutes. Add the plantains, then pour in the chicken stock and bring to a boil. Lower the heat to a simmer and cook until the plantains are very soft, 30 to 40 minutes.

Puree the soup in the pot using an immersion blender or carefully transfer it in batches to a regular blender. Stir in the lime juice and cumin and add salt and pepper to taste. Serve hot, topped with Crispy Shallots.

CRISPY SHALLOTS

MAKES ABOUT ¾ CUP

1 cup cornstarch

1 teaspoon salt

3 shallots, sliced into ⅛-inch-thick rings

About 1 quart canola or grapeseed oil

Mix the cornstarch and salt in a large bowl. Add the shallots and toss to coat them in the cornstarch mixture. Using a spider, remove the shallots from the bowl, shaking off the excess cornstarch.

Place the shallots in a saucepan and pour in enough oil to cover them by about 2 inches. The oil should not be higher than half-way up the sides of the saucepan. Swirl the oil and shallots gently to get rid of any air pockets, but don't stir them with a spoon; you

risk scraping the cornstarch off the shallots.

Place the pan over medium-low heat and let it heat slowly. Depending on the size of your pan, slow-frying the shallots can take anywhere from 20 to 40 minutes. Keep a close eye on the shallots. The moment the shallots begin to take on any golden color, scoop them out of the hot oil with a spider and transfer them to paper towels to drain. Sprinkle them with a little more salt.

This is not your grandmother's chicken soup and dumpling recipe, unless you're fortunate enough to have a Cuban grandmother. With its long simmering time and the addition of calabaza, the tiny orange-and-white squash, this is a wonderful way to warm up a crisp autumn day. The addition of Bijol (see page 7) infuses the soup with a pleasing yellow color, but if you don't have a Latin specialty market in the neighborhood or don't have time for mail order, a pinch of turmeric makes a good substitute. The plantain dumplings are a lovely combination of sweet and savory, but they do not hold well. If you have leftover soup, the dumplings will completely disintegrate overnight. If you are not planning to eat all the soup in one go, add only enough dumplings to suit your hunger pangs, then freeze the soup without dumplings and whip them up whenever you're ready to dive into the leftovers.

SOPA DE POLLO
WITH PLANTAIN DUMPLINGS

SERVES 6 TO 8

3 boneless, skinless chicken breasts

1 yellow onion, diced

2 celery stalks, sliced ½ inch thick

2 carrots, sliced ½ inch thick

4 cloves garlic, sliced paper-thin

10 cups Chicken Stock (page 16)

2 cups calabaza squash, cut into 1-inch dice

2 tomatoes, diced

½ teaspoon ground cumin

½ teaspoon Bijol (optional, for color)

2 ripe plantains, peeled

2 teaspoons water

½ teaspoon salt, more to taste

¼ teaspoon freshly ground pepper, more to taste

2 tablespoons chopped fresh parsley

Place the chicken, onion, celery, carrots, and garlic in a large pot and pour in the chicken stock. Bring to a boil, then reduce the heat to low and simmer for 25 minutes.

Remove the chicken from the pot and let it cool slightly. Shred the chicken with two forks, and add it back to the soup. Add the calabaza, tomatoes, cumin, and Bijol. Continue simmering for 10 to 15 minutes, until the calabaza is tender.

While the soup simmers, place the plantains in a microwave-safe bowl with the water and cover it tightly with plastic wrap. Microwave for 2 minutes, until very soft. (If you don't have a microwave, place the plantains in a skillet with ⅓ cup water, cover with a tight-fitting lid, and cook over medium heat until the plantains are softened, 12 to 15 minutes. Less water is better—the plantains' sweetness will leach out into excess water.) Sprinkle the plantains with the salt and pepper and mash them with a fork. Roll the mashed plantain into small, smooth balls about 1 inch in diameter.

Drop the plantain dumplings into the soup and cook for 10 more minutes. Remove the soup from the heat, season it to taste with salt and pepper, and stir in the chopped parsley. Serve immediately.

SPICY BLACK BEAN SOUP

Soaking the beans with their aromatics overnight imbues them with flavors that are further enhanced by the ingredients added in the stewing process. The soaking liquid from the beans serves as the basis for the soup, and your palate will thank you for the additional layers of flavors that it delivers. Don't be shy about drizzling a hefty dose of the Lime Crema onto your soup. It brightens it and adds a pleasing creamy finish.

SPICY BLACK BEAN SOUP
WITH LIME CREMA

SERVES 8 TO 10

1 pound dried black beans

1 yellow onion, peeled and halved

1 green bell pepper, stemmed, halved, and seeded

2 bay leaves

2 teaspoons salt

¼ cup olive oil

1 large yellow onion, diced

1 green bell pepper, stemmed, seeded, and diced

2 jalapeños, stemmed, seeded, and diced

4 cloves garlic, minced

2 cups Chicken Stock (page 16)

1 teaspoon dried oregano

1 teaspoon ground cumin

1 tablespoon sugar

1 tablespoon red wine vinegar

Freshly ground pepper

1 cup Lime Crema (see recipe)

Put the beans, the halved onion, the halved pepper, and the bay leaves in a large pot and cover with water by at least 3 inches. Place the pot in the refrigerator overnight.

Pour the beans and their soaking liquid into a large pot. Make sure the water covers the beans by 1 inch, adding or removing water if necessary. Bring the water to a boil, then lower the heat to simmer until the beans are tender, 45 to 55 minutes. Stir in the salt.

Let the beans continue to simmer while you make the sofrito. Heat the oil in a large skillet over medium heat. Add the diced onion, bell pepper, and jalapeños and cook until softened, 8 to 10 minutes. Stir in the garlic and cook until fragrant, about 2 minutes more. Stir the sofrito into the beans.

Remove the now-mushy halved onion and pepper and the bay leaves from the bean pot and discard the bay leaves. Place the vegetables in a blender and ladle in about 2 cups of the beans. Puree the beans and vegetables. Stir this puree back into the beans in the pot. Add the chicken stock. Bring the soup to a simmer and add the oregano, cumin, sugar, and vinegar. Simmer for 30 minutes. Add salt and pepper to taste. Serve hot with a dollop of Lime Crema.

LIME CREMA

MAKES 1 CUP

1 cup Mexican crema
3 tablespoons freshly
squeezed lime juice
1 teaspoon lime zest
Salt

Whisk together all of the ingredients except the salt. Season to taste with salt. Refrigerate the crema until ready to serve.

CREAM OF MALANGA SOUP

Yuda Cardova, a naturalist at the Parque Nacional Vinales, told us that "in Cuba, the first thing you're given to eat when you're born is malanga, for its healthful benefits." The tuberous root that is sold as malanga in Cuba is actually not malanga, but taro root. Both have starchy white flesh and belong to the same family, but they are from different plant genera. But Yuda was not wrong about its nutritional benefits. Taro can aid digestion and is said to combat certain types of cancers, decrease blood pressure, and support the immune system. This soup is a lovely way to gain the health benefits of "Cuban malanga." The Pistachio Pistou makes a tempting garnish that is also fantastic drizzled over a hunk of sourdough bread.

CREAM OF MALANGA SOUP WITH PISTACHIO PISTOU

SERVES 4 TO 6

2 tablespoons olive oil

1 yellow onion, chopped

4 cloves garlic, coarsely chopped

2 pounds malanga or taro, peeled and cut into 1-inch chunks

4 cups Chicken Stock (page 16)

½ cup heavy cream

1 teaspoon white pepper

Salt

Pistachio Pistou (see recipe)

Heat the olive oil in a large pot over medium heat until it just begins to shimmer. Add the onion and cook until softened but not browned, about 8 minutes. Add the garlic and cook for 2 more minutes, stirring occasionally.

Add the malanga and the stock. Cover and bring to a boil, then reduce the heat and simmer until the malanga is very soft, about 30 minutes. Carefully blend the soup until it is smooth, using either an immersion blender or a standard blender. Stir in the heavy cream, white pepper, and salt to taste. Serve with a dollop of Pistachio Pistou.

PISTACHIO PISTOU

MAKES ABOUT ¾ CUP

½ cup shelled unsalted
pistachios
2 cloves garlic, peeled
1 teaspoon lemon zest
½ cup chopped fresh parsley
½ cup olive oil
Salt and freshly ground pepper

Pulse the pistachios in a food processor until coarsely chopped. Transfer the pistachios to a bowl, then drop the garlic, one clove at a time, into the food processor with the motor running. Stop the machine and add the lemon zest and parsley. Process until coarsely chopped, then scrape the mixture into the bowl with the pistachios. Stir in the olive oil and season to taste with salt and pepper.

This robust fisherman's stew reflects the seafaring tradition of Cuba. It's a briny one-pot wonder, prepared with whichever firm white fish looks best at your fishmonger's that day. If you're feeling festive, add a handful of peeled and deveined shrimp near the end of the cooking process and simmer them until their flesh turns pink. Garnish with chopped scallions and a dollop of sour cream along with a squeeze of lime.

FISHER-MAN'S STEW

SERVES 6 TO 8

2 tablespoons olive oil

1 yellow onion, chopped

1 green bell pepper, stemmed, seeded, and chopped

2 celery stalks, sliced ½ inch thick

4 cloves garlic, minced

Salt

6 cups Fish Stock (page 20)

1 (28-ounce) can crushed tomatoes

½ cup dry white wine

1 teaspoon Bijol

2 bay leaves

2 cups peeled, diced russet potatoes

2 pounds firm white fish, such as cod or halibut, cut in to 2-inch cubes

3 tablespoons chopped fresh parsley

Lime wedges, for serving

Heat the oil in a large pot over medium heat until just shimmering. Add the onion, bell pepper, and celery and sauté for 5 to 10 minutes, until beginning to soften. Add the garlic and a healthy pinch of salt and cook until fragrant, 2 to 3 more minutes.

Add the fish stock, tomatoes, wine, Bijol, and bay leaves. Bring the mixture to a boil, then lower the heat to a simmer and add the potatoes. Cook until the potatoes are tender, about 20 minutes. Taste and add salt if necessary (it really depends on how much salt there is in your fish stock).

Add the fish and cook until it is firm and opaque throughout, 8 to 10 minutes. Remove the stew from the heat, stir in the chopped parsley, and serve with lime wedges on the side.

There's little indication remaining in Barrio Chino de La Habana, Havana's Chinatown, that this was once the largest Chinatown in Latin America. There is in fact only one Chinese chef still cooking in this minuscule neighborhood, formerly one of the city's liveliest districts. We met Chef Shugui Luo at Tien Tan, the sole restaurant in Havana that still serves authentic Chinese cuisine—or as close to authentic as can be achieved with limited supplies.

Chef Luo first invited us to cook with him in a kitchen at the back of his establishment festooned with red paper lanterns and golden dragons parading across its walls. All his staff members were Cubans; they good-naturedly teased their boss, who in turn stole their chef hats, waving them above his head until they apologized for their jokes. Once Chef Luo started tossing food in his massive wok, filled with daikon and shiitakes laced with mirin and chili sauce, over a blazing flame, the humor subsided and it was all about the business of cooking. He finished off the dish with plump, glistening shrimp before meeting with us in his dining room to explain how he became the only Chinese chef cooking in Havana.

The Chinese began to arrive in Cuba in the mid-nineteenth century in response to unrest among the nation's African slave population. Their initial role was to work alongside African slaves; after slavery was abolished in Cuba in 1886, the Chinese filled the spots in the cane and coffee fields that the Africans had vacated. Cuba was the first nation to receive Chinese citizens who were indentured servants, required to serve an eight-year work sentence before gaining their independence as payment for their transport from China to Cuba.

Throughout the next century, over 120,000 arrived in Cuba on government contracts, bringing with them food traditions such as dumplings and chow mein that still linger in the Cuban culinary lexicon.

Even when their numbers in the sugarcane fields waned—a result of the labor trade to Cuba being prohibited by China, due to contract breaches and abuse by Cuban plantation owners—the Chinese population maintained a prominent presence. Chinatown buzzed with industry in the ensuing years, and since the majority of the

dim sum
a little r

Chinese who traveled to Cuba were men, there were also many marriages between Chinese men and Cuban women, with many Cuban-Chinese offspring. The Chinese also brought with them Buddhism, and while the religion was never as dominant as Christianity or Santeria in Cuba, it did influence a small population of Cubans drawn to its advocacy of compassion and benevolence.

The Chinese fought valiantly alongside their Cuban counterparts during the Ten Years' War to gain independence from Spain. A monument was erected in Havana to honor these soldiers, still viewed today as national heroes. The Revolution affected the Chinese and Cuban-Chinese citizens of Cuba in profound and detrimental ways. When the government began nationalizing their restaurants and stores, many of the Chinese business owners fled for other parts of the Caribbean and the United States, significantly reducing their population in Cuba and decimating Havana's once thriving Chinatown.

Shugui Luo is not a descendent of this first wave of Chinese immigration; he arrived sixteen years ago from the Chinese province of Xiong Xi. He explained to us that he knew the restaurant owner, who convinced him that there were many opportunities in Havana for a Chinese chef like himself. He paused for a long time, looking down at a plate of garnishes that included limes and avocados. "I'm not sure yet if it was a good move. Only time will tell."

"But it has been sixteen years already. Hasn't the answer already revealed itself?"

"You discover when you move to Cuba that it can be a confusing place. I learned to accept this and came to understand that sometimes the answers you seek never materialize. It's something I have to accept."

"Is there anything else that you've learned to accept?"

"Yes. In my part of China we eat Cantonese cuisine, which is very spicy. I miss cooking with heat, but it is my hope that with this change that is now taking place in the country, the Cuban palate might change too, becoming more accepting, more open to new flavors and new ideas."

CRAB DUMPLINGS
WITH CILANTRO DIPPING SAUCE

SERVES 12 TO 14

1 pound fresh crab meat, picked through for shells

½ cup diced green bell pepper

2 tablespoons minced jalapeño

6 green onions, white and green parts, finely chopped

2 teaspoons freshly squeezed lemon juice

⅓ cup mayonnaise

1 teaspoon salt

½ teaspoon freshly ground pepper

50 wonton wrappers

Vegetable oil for deep-frying

Cilantro Dipping Sauce (see recipe)

Mix the crab, bell pepper, jalapeño, green onion, lemon juice, mayonnaise, salt, and pepper in a large bowl. Set aside.

Set up your workspace: Line a baking sheet with parchment paper. Cover it with a clean, slightly damp dish towel and set it nearby. You will place your finished dumplings under this towel to keep them from drying out and cracking. You will also need a small bowl of water for sealing the dumplings.

Spoon about 1 teaspoon of filling into the center of a wonton wrapper. Dip a finger in the water and moisten the edges of the wrapper. Fold the wrapper over the mixture, making a plump triangle. Press the edges together tightly to seal the dumpling. Place the finished dumpling under the damp dish towel and repeat with the remaining wonton wrappers and filling.

When you have finished filling all of the dumplings, heat at least 4 inches of vegetable oil in a heavy saucepan over medium-high heat until it reaches 375°F. Fry 4 to 6 dumplings at a time, turning to fry all sides evenly, until they are golden brown, 4 to 5 minutes per batch. Transfer the fried dumplings to paper towels to drain. Serve hot with Cilantro Dipping Sauce.

CILANTRO DIPPING SAUCE

MAKES ABOUT ¾ CUP

2 cloves garlic, peeled

1 jalapeño, stemmed and seeded

2 cups coarsely chopped fresh cilantro

3 tablespoons unseasoned rice wine vinegar

1 teaspoon salt

¼ teaspoon freshly ground pepper

½ cup extra-virgin olive oil

Place the garlic and jalapeño in a food processor and pulse until finely chopped. Add the cilantro, vinegar, salt, and pepper and process, pausing once to scrape down the sides, until a smooth paste forms. With the machine running, slowly stream in the oil. Taste and adjust the seasoning, if necessary.

This recipe gracefully combines the culinary traditions of two nations by enveloping crab, a Caribbean mainstay, in a quintessentially Chinese wonton wrapper, deep-fried to a golden crunch. Don't let the prospect of assembling wontons scare you off. They're actually a breeze to prepare. The only trick is ensuring that the wrappers are covered with a damp cloth during every step of the development process. Also, be sure to fry in small batches to avoid overcrowding, and once they begin to turn brown, remove from the oil and drain on paper towels. They will continue to brown up after they have been removed from the oil, so removing them just as they begin to turn a light caramel hue will prevent overcooking and burnt edges. The Cilantro Dipping Sauce adds a zing to the fried coating.

CUCHILLO STREET EGG ROLLS

Cuchillo Street is essentially all that remains of Chinatown in Havana's Central District. It's a nostalgic reminder of what was once a thriving district where restaurants served up a distinctive blend of Cuban-Chinese cuisine. These egg rolls represent that long-lost union of two seemingly disparate cultures that when melded, formed something wondrously appealing in its distinctiveness. The chorizo and black beans are the stars of this egg roll show and will surprise guests with their unexpected presence. Combine them with cabbage, peppers, and an egg roll wrapper fried to golden brown, and you'll have a hit of instant nostalgia that will remind any Cuban old enough to remember of those glory days when Havana's Chinatown was an intriguing hub of industry and passion.

CUCHILLO STREET EGG ROLLS

SERVES 12

2 heads napa cabbage, cored and shredded

3 carrots, shredded

2 red finger hot chiles or jalapeños, stemmed, seeded, and chopped (Choose finger hots if you can take the heat—jalapeños are a milder option.)

1 cup ¼-inch-diced Spanish-style chorizo

1 cup tiny (salad-size) cooked shrimp or chopped cooked shrimp of any size

1 cup ¼-inch-diced cooked ham

1 cup cooked black beans

2 tablespoons vegetable oil

2 teaspoons sesame oil

2 teaspoons salt

2 teaspoons sugar

1 egg

1 tablespoon water

1 (1-pound) package egg roll wrappers

Vegetable oil for deep-frying

Bottled sweet chili dipping sauce

Bring a large pot of salted water to a boil and prepare an ice-water bath. Add the cabbage and carrots to the boiling water and cook for 2 to 3 minutes. Using a fine-mesh strainer, transfer the vegetables to the ice-water bath. When the vegetables are cold, strain them from the ice water and use your hands to squeeze out as much liquid as possible. Leave the vegetables in the strainer to continue draining while you prep everything else. Drained to avoid making the egg rolls soggy.

Mix the chiles, chorizo, shrimp, ham, black beans, vegetable oil, sesame oil, salt, and sugar in a large bowl. Check on the cabbage and carrots to ensure that they are dry. If they still feel damp, spread a clean dish towel on your work surface and lay the vegetables in the center. Roll up the dish towel and twist it firmly to force out any remaining liquid. Add the dry cabbage and carrots to the other ingredients and mix.

Lightly beat together the egg and water in a small bowl. Lay one egg roll wrapper on a clean work surface with one corner pointing toward you. Spoon about 3 table-spoons of filling onto the bottom half of the diamond, using your fingers to push it into a horizontal log shape. Using a pastry brush, brush egg wash around the edge of the wrapper in a 1-inch border. To roll the egg roll, fold the bottom point up, fold in both sides, then continue rolling up from the bottom to seal. Repeat with the remaining wrappers and filling.

Heat at least 4 inches of vegetable oil in a heavy pot until it reaches 350°F. Working in batches, fry the egg rolls until golden brown all over, flipping as necessary. Remove them from the oil using a spider or slotted spoon and drain on paper towels. Serve them hot with sweet chili dipping sauce.

This is a straightforward fried rice recipe in that all of the hallowed ingredients—such as eggs, ginger, scallions, soy sauce, and chiles—are present, but they get their marching orders from the Cuban mainstays of chorizo and shrimp. It's a fun mashup of the two cultures certain to win over your family on a night when you want to wow them without overextending yourself in the kitchen.

CUBAN FRIED RICE

SERVES 4 TO 6

3 tablespoons vegetable oil, divided

½ yellow onion, diced

½ green bell pepper, stemmed, seeded, and diced

3 cloves garlic, minced

1 tablespoon minced ginger

1 cup diced Spanish-style chorizo

1 cup small raw shrimp, peeled, deveined, tails removed

1 cup diced cooked lean pork, such as from leftover chops or loin roast

3 cups cooked long-grain rice, chilled

2 tablespoons soy sauce

2 teaspoons Sriracha sauce

2 eggs, scrambled and set aside

½ cup chopped green onions, white and green parts

2 tablespoons chopped fresh cilantro

Heat 1 tablespoon of the oil in a large skillet over medium-high heat and sauté the onion and bell pepper until slightly browned, 7 to 9 minutes. Add the garlic and ginger and cook until fragrant, about 2 more minutes. Add the chorizo, shrimp, and pork. Cook until the shrimp are no longer translucent, 4 to 5 minutes. Transfer the mixture to a large bowl and return the pan to the heat.

Add the remaining 2 tablespoons oil to the hot pan, then add the rice and stir to coat it with oil. Cook for 5 minutes, stirring occasionally, then return the vegetables and meat to the pan. Stir in the soy and Sriracha sauces, along with the scrambled eggs, green onions, and cilantro. Serve hot.

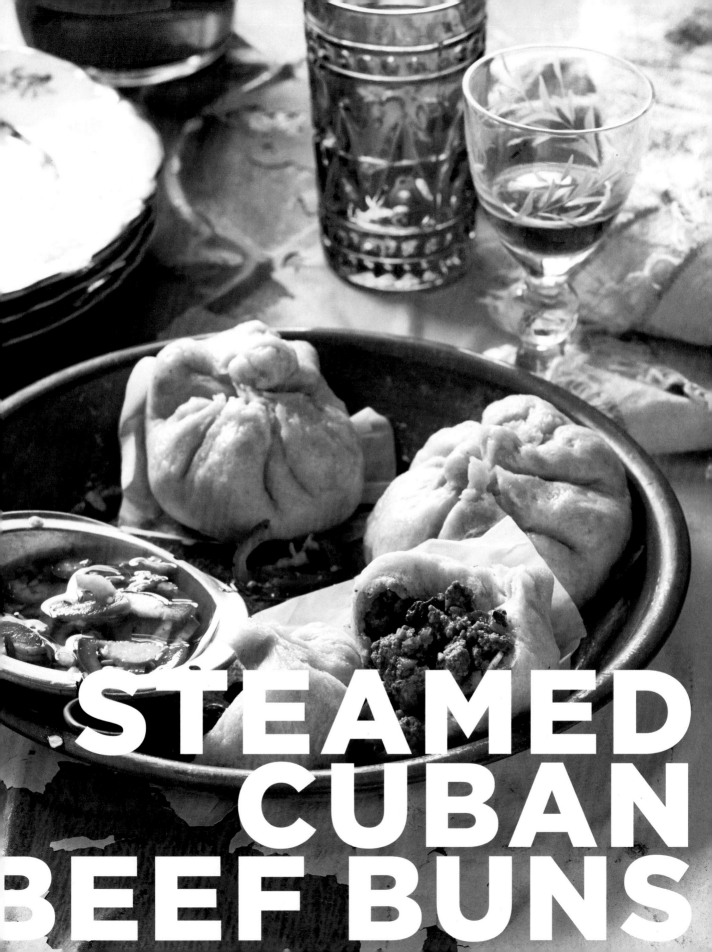

STEAMED CUBAN BEEF BUNS

If you have a steamer and parchment paper and are comfortable working with yeast, please do dive into this recipe with abandon. It's a tempting marriage of a Chinese tradition and Cuban flavors that will prove virtually irresistible for anyone who catches a whiff of the cumin- and cinnamon-scented air it conjures. Dried currants add a chewy sweetness to the robust blend of beef and spices, and cilantro and vinegar give it the kick in the pants that any Cuban grandmother would appreciate.

STEAMED CUBAN BEEF BUNS

SERVES 6 TO 8

DOUGH

1 cup lukewarm water

2 teaspoons fast-acting yeast

2 tablespoons sugar

1 teaspoon salt

2 tablespoons plus 2 teaspoons vegetable oil, divided

3 cups all-purpose flour, divided

2 teaspoons baking powder

FILLING

2 tablespoons vegetable oil

1 pound ground beef

½ white onion, diced

½ red bell pepper, stemmed, seeded, and diced

4 cloves garlic, minced

2 teaspoons minced fresh ginger

½ cup dried currants

1 teaspoon cumin

¼ teaspoon ground cinnamon

½ teaspoon crushed red pepper

1 teaspoon salt

2 tablespoons white vinegar

⅓ cup Chicken Stock (page 16)

¼ cup chopped fresh cilantro

To make the dough, pour the water into a large mixing bowl and sprinkle in the yeast and sugar. Let the mixture stand for 5 minutes, then add the salt, 2 tablespoons of the vegetable oil, and 2 cups of the flour. Stir with a wooden spoon until the dough is homogenous, then add the remaining 1 cup of flour. Stir in the flour as best you can, then turn out the dough onto a clean work surface and knead it until it is completely smooth and elastic, 12 to 15 minutes. Alternatively, place the dough in the bowl of a stand mixer fitted with the dough hook attachment and knead on low speed for 7 to 8 minutes.

Pour the remaining 2 teaspoons oil into the bowl in which you mixed the dough. Place the dough ball in the bowl, turning it to coat all sides with oil. Cover the bowl with a clean kitchen towel and leave it in a warm place. Let the dough rise until it has doubled in size, 45 minutes to 1 hour.

Punch down the dough and turn it out onto a lightly floured work surface. Sprinkle the baking powder over the dough and knead it in until it is fully incorporated. Let the dough rest for 20 minutes while you prepare the filling.

To make the filling, heat the oil in a large skillet over medium heat. Add the ground beef and cook until lightly browned, breaking up the chunks with a spatula or wooden spoon. Remove the pan from the heat and scoop out the beef, leaving any rendered fat behind. Pour out all but 1 tablespoon of fat, return the skillet to medium heat, and add the onion and bell pepper. Cook until softened, 8 to 10 minutes. Add the garlic and ginger and cook, stirring, for 2 more minutes.

Return the beef to the skillet and stir in the currants, cumin, cinnamon, crushed red pepper, salt, vinegar, and stock. Bring the mixture to a simmer and cook for about 10 minutes. Remove from the heat and stir in the cilantro. Let the mixture cool before assembling the buns.

Working on a lightly floured surface, divide the dough into 16 equal pieces and roll them into balls. Cut sixteen 3-inch squares from parchment paper. These will be placed underneath the buns so they don't stick during the steaming process. Roll out each dough ball into a circle 4 inches in diameter. Place the dough circle in the palm of your hand and spoon 2 tablespoons of the filling into the center. Gather the edges of the circle up around the meat mixture, pinching the top closed. Place the bun on a parchment square, pinched side up.

Heat about 3 cups of water in a large steamer. Place the buns in the steamer about 1 inch apart so they don't stick together, and steam for 25 minutes. Serve hot.

This recipe sounds complicated and luxurious but it's actually a breeze to prepare. It's one to keep in mind when you want to impress your guests without having to fret over a complicated recipe. Consider it the grown-up version of pork and beans, Cuban style, with a little Chinese influence thrown in for good measure. The secret is to keep spooning the marinade over the pork as it cooks, allowing it to absorb until it finally transforms into a sticky glaze—a "can't get enough of it" kind of finish.

HAVANESE PORK LOIN

SERVES 6 TO 8

¼ cup cooked black beans
¼ cup hoisin sauce
2 tablespoons soy sauce
2 teaspoons dry cooking sherry
3 tablespoons sugar
3 cloves garlic, minced
1 teaspoon five-spice powder
1 (2- to 4-pound) boneless pork loin roast
White Rice (page 14)

Preheat the oven to 425°F. Place the black beans in a small bowl and mash them with a fork. Stir in the hoisin sauce, soy sauce, sherry, sugar, garlic, and five-spice powder. Rub about ¼ cup of the marinade over the pork and place the pork on a rack over a roasting pan. Pour ½ of water into the pan.

Roast for 15 minutes, then lower the oven temperature to 350°F and continue roasting until the internal temperature reaches 155°F, spooning additional marinade over the pork every 15 minutes or so.

Remove the pork from the oven. Let it rest for 15 minutes before slicing and serving with white rice.

We ate a version of this dish when we visited Havana's Chinatown (see page 146). At that restaurant it was served with a plate of avocados and lime, reminding us that even though our meal was prepared by a native Chinese chef, no matter how much we felt transported to China on this minuscule thread of a street, with nostalgic reminders of its heyday lingering in every corner, we were still in Cuba. Be sure to clean your lobsters of any residue before chopping them into large chunks that will readily absorb the sweet-and-sour sauce. If you're looking for a little extra spark to get your Cuban-Chinese lobster party started, add a little chopped jalapeño to the sauce before cooking it.

SWEET-AND-SOUR LOBSTER

SERVES 6

3 (1- to 1½-pound) live lobsters

1 tablespoon vegetable oil

1 large yellow onion, thinly sliced

2 green bell peppers, stemmed, seeded, and cut into 1-inch dice

1 pineapple, peeled, cored, and cut into 1-inch dice

3 tablespoons cornstarch

½ cup cold water

1½ cups pineapple juice

¼ cup white vinegar

3 tablespoons soy sauce

2 tablespoons brown sugar

White Rice (page 14)

Bring a large pot of salted water to a rolling boil and add the lobsters. Depending on the size of your pot, you might need to cook the lobsters in more than one batch to avoid lowering the water temperature and losing the boil. Cover the pot and cook for 8 to 12 minutes, until the lobsters are red and cooked through. The lobsters should cook for about 8 minutes per pound, so adjust the time up or down based on the size of your lobsters. Use tongs to remove the lobsters from the pot and set them aside to cool.

Crack the shells, using a lobster cracker or the back edge of a chef's knife, and pick all the meat out of the lobsters. Chop the meat into bite-size chunks.

Heat the oil in a large skillet over medium heat and add the onion and peppers. Sauté until the vegetables begin to soften. Add the pineapple and chopped lobster meat and toss to combine. Set aside.

To make the sauce, whisk the cornstarch and water in a small bowl and set aside. Bring the pineapple juice, vinegar, soy sauce, and brown sugar to a boil in a small saucepan, then add the cornstarch slurry 1 tablespoon at a time, stirring constantly. When the sauce is thickened to your liking, pour it over the cooked vegetables and lobster and stir to coat everything. Serve with white rice.

Cuba turned out to be much bigger than we expected, and when we hit the road we discovered that vestiges of indigenous people's cuisine can still be found—and savored—in its remote corners. The food in the rural areas also features a wider array of ingredients than we found in Havana, since the city's culinary repertoire is primarily quick-fix recipes made with commodity foods.

There's nothing like speeding along the highway in a vintage car to one of Cuba's outlying areas. One of our first stops was in Hershey, an eerie ghost town named after the American chocolate factory that thrived here before the Revolution. The government is not keen on visitors to Hershey, and we had to explore the area covertly so as not to attract unwelcome government minders. The first thing we noticed was the silence, then the skeletons of decaying buildings that once hummed with industry. A tattered Cuban flag fluttered in the wind next to train tracks partially obscured by drifting sand. There was a single train car clinging to the rusting rails. After wandering around for a while, our hunger intensifying, we bumped into a local. When we explained how ravenous we were, he told us about a woman who cooked local cuisine for the town's remaining workers.

We knocked on the door of a train car he directed us to and were greeted by a voluptuous Afro-Cuban woman with a robust belly laugh and infectious spirit, who invited us into her makeshift home. She proudly displayed a collection of threadbare stuffed animals hanging from the ceiling. There were around a dozen other beds scattered throughout the train cars, along with a few hammocks for the remaining workers to sleep on. Behind the train, the woman tended to several enormous pots bubbling with stews and other one-pot delicacies whose fragrance made our stomachs rumble.

She shared with us her tale and the story of the people who used to live in Hershey when it was a vital component of the Cuban economy. Once it was a place of opportunity where one of earth's sweetest offerings was crafted by employees who viewed the future with unbridled optimism, the taste of chocolate sugar-coating their mouths and their dreams.

We will never forget her vivacious demeanor and incredible laughter or the flavorful bowls of congri and chicken stew that she served to us. Bidding a reluctant farewell to our new friend—and stellar cook—we headed off on our next adventure.

all aboa

We discovered the same sort of buoyant optimism at the next stop on our road trip at Santa Maria Beach, where turquoise blue waves lapped the sugar-white sand. Less than an hour outside of Havana, this is where the locals, and an ever-growing tourist population, go to exchange the madness of the city for an idyllic tropical retreat, complete with beach umbrellas and cerulean waves that crest in a soothing staccato against the shore.

The beach seems destined to become an overcrowded tourist hot spot in years to come, but for now it's an escape affording a dreamy day fueled by grilled snapper and fried plantains. We spent an entire afternoon with our friend Pepe and driver Roberto with our shoes off, digging our toes into the hot sand, watching a vendor carry his tray of rum-filled coconuts adeptly on his shoulder up and down the seven-and-a-half-mile stretch of beach. Our lunch concluded with a music session of Cuban classics performed by a mariachi band complete with a bass guitar; after a few more rum-filled coconuts, we felt confident enough to play the maracas alongside.

Somewhere in between the sad remains of Hershey and the bliss of Santa Maria lies Viñales, a region in western Cuba about three hours from Havana whose fertile valleys produce the nation's famed tobacco and boast some of its first independently owned organic farms (see page 170).

On the road, far from Havana, we tasted dishes reflecting the food traditions of the indigenous Cuban population that were decimated by the Spaniards. It is also beyond Havana that ingredients like rabbit, goat, and lamb are more commonly enjoyed by the local population and frequently appear on restaurant menus. The cuisine is more nuanced in the countryside, shaped less by government rations than by the fresh ingredients growing in orchards, farms, and gardens.

tobacco

"We don't know anything else. We are like children, and the government has clever ways of suppressing us." Paco, a fourth-generation tobacco farmer in the Viñales Valley, pinched a bundle of tobacco leaves hanging from the rafters of his drying house to test their moisture content between his thick, leathery fingers. We were surrounded by thousands of these bundles, and we couldn't help but feel the envy of cigar connoisseurs the world over who covet a visit to the most famed tobacco- production region on the planet.

Paco was in his fifties; a cowboy hat shaded his handsome, angular face. To explain the leaf variations required to construct a cigar, he took one from his pocket and deconstructed it into three layers. There's the *capa*, the outer layer that he said must be visually appealing for an elegant finish. Beneath it is the *capote*, a binder made from the lower portion of the tobacco leaf. Inside is the *tripa*, whose primary requirement is that it be combustible. We were to learn on subsequent days in Vinales how laborious and time-consuming the cigar-making process is, but in the company of Paco, we learned primarily about the agony of the tobacco farmer.

"All of the tobacco farms are nationalized," Paco explained as he walked down the line of hanging bundles to test each one for moisture. "The government delivers tobacco seed to us; we are required to grow it, and they collect the leaves after they are sufficiently dried. The locals are allowed to use only what is deemed unacceptable by the government."

We were fairly certain that Cuban cigars would never hold the same tantalizing allure that they once did, now that we knew their sale benefited no one but the government and that the tobacco farmers who painstakingly grew and processed the leaves would most likely never smoke a high-quality Cuban cigar. Those are all exported, except for the very few that find their way into the Cuban black market.

Before departing, we asked Paco what was most challenging about being a tobacco farmer. He looked down at his dusty boots for a few moments before responding, "Everything is a challenge in this work. The worst of it is remembering what used to be." And he waved farewell to us from the door of his drying house.

Many of the farms in Vinales have been in the same family for six or seven generations, long enough for the stories passed down from one generation to the next to remind the current family of the freedom their ancestors once had and the pride they took in growing tobacco leaves. Today, most of the farms grow leaves for a single tobacco company, and the production is strictly monitored by government officials.

At another drying house in the valley, the tobacco leaves were being transferred from their *cujes*, or drying sticks, to neatly arranged piles on the ground where they would continue to dry for another few months before being transported to one of five production centers in Vinales. Once the leaves are flattened, they are wrapped in palm leaves, a step that creates a natural humidor, enabling the leaves to begin their fermentation process. This particular house contained over eleven thousand tobacco leaves, their earthy aroma filling our noses as an intense ammonia filled our eyes, leaving them stinging and watery.

We learned from José, an Afro-Cuban who asked us not to use his last name, that tobacco seeds are planted in October; they grow for the next three months, reaching three feet in height before the January harvest. A cigar dangled from José's cracked lip, his weathered fingers deftly rolling another cigar for his personal use. He told us he was now thirty-nine and had been smoking since he was ten years old. Then he shared his best piece of advice for rolling cigars: "Cigars are just like women. If you squeeze them too much, they break. You need a gentle hand to keep them happy. Other than that, soil and climate are the next most important things. But the way you handle them always comes first." We asked him if he ever cooks with tobacco leaves; he said no, but explained that they sometimes soak the leaves in honey before wrapping and smoking them.

At a tobacco production center on the outskirts of the valley, we learned about the final steps in the cigar-making process. We were overwhelmed: there are approximately 125 actions required to transform a raw leaf into one suitable for smoking. Nearly sixty women worked industriously at small wooden tables arranged neatly on the floor of the massive production center. A humid wind blew through the open windows, filling our noses with the potent aroma of tobacco as the sound of the room filled with the voice of the reader, a woman hired to read to the employees from a table laden with books and periodicals. It helps to quell boredom while educating them at the same time.

Helena Abrantes, a middle-aged woman with a confident nature and knowing eyes, offered us a tour of the production facility; she became its overseer after nearly two decades of working as a leaf processor. As we strolled slowly past the tiny tables of industrious women, she explained that 70 percent of the nicotine is contained in the leaf itself, but the stem contains an even higher concentration; it is stripped from the leaf because it would otherwise overpower the cigar.

The women discarded the stems on the floor; Helena explained they would be recycled to use as either fertilizer or pesticide or to lace perfume with subtle tobacco notes. Once the leaves are processed, they are bound for at least one year to continue the fermentation process begun in the drying houses. Any broken leaves are used in cigarettes and pipes. Aromatics are sometimes added before the fermentation process continues, if specified by the particular cigar company they are being prepared for. Fermentation develops the flavor and aroma of the tobacco, coaxing out its virtues over the course of several months.

Once ready, the leaves are transferred to a heating room where they are refined for a further six to eight hours, resulting in an intense release of ammonia that forced us to cover our eyes as they filled with tears. The leaves are then wrapped in palm leaves once more to form neat bundles and labeled with all relevant origin and processing information before being sent to the appropriate warehouse, where they are aged for an additional three to four years before finally being incorporated into a cigar.

Later that day in Pinar del Rio, the main town of Vinales, we decided there couldn't be a more appropriate place to indulge in a Cuban marriage: a union that includes a shot of rum finished off with a puff on a cigar and a swig of espresso. As the caramel notes of the rum mingled with the honeyed flavor of the cigar and bitterness of the coffee, we thought of Helena, who relished explaining the entire process to her rapt audience and clearly took great pride in her work—justifiably so. It was astounding to think of what each leaf went through before earning its place in a cigar coveted the world over, and we now understood why they were so valuable, while at the same time lamenting the absence of the highest-quality cigars in the lives of the farmers who toiled beneath the scorching sun to grow them.

FRIED WHOLE SNAPPER

There are several species of snapper in Cuba. The cubera, mutton, and sailfin varieties are the most notable, but since they can be difficult to source, we're using a common red snapper in this recipe (yellowtail also works). Snapper was the fish we enjoyed while listening to a mariachi band on Santa Maria Beach (see page 165), and we now enjoy the dish all the more because it reminds us of the dazzling turquoise blue water that was our backdrop that day. The salsa verde is prepared using capers and parsley along with a copious amount of lemon juice, all of which elevate this fish by cutting through its fried crust with a zesty dose of flavor. Note: If you are planning to fry whole snapper (either red or yellowtail), you'll need to make some serious preparations—it requires a lot of oil and either a deep-fryer or a large, deep skillet big enough to submerge the fish in oil without the oil boiling over. One tip is to snip off its tail before frying; that will buy you around an inch more space.

FRIED WHOLE SNAPPER WITH SALSA VERDE

SERVES 4

Vegetable oil for deep-frying
2½ teaspoons salt, divided
1 teaspoon granulated garlic
1 teaspoon dried oregano
½ teaspoon freshly ground black pepper
1 cup all-purpose flour
2 to 4 whole red or yellowtail snapper (depending on size of fish), scaled, gutted, and cleaned
Salsa Verde (see recipe)

Begin heating at least 4 inches of oil in a large, heavy pot (wide enough to fit the fish) over medium-high heat. The oil must reach 360° to 365°F before frying.

Mix 1½ teaspoons of the salt with the granulated garlic, oregano, and pepper in a small bowl.

Combine the flour and the remaining 1 teaspoon salt in a pie pan or shallow dish. Make three diagonal slashes on each side of each fish and sprinkle the fish with the spice mix, both inside and out.

When the oil has come up to temperature, dredge one of the fish in the flour mixture, shaking off the excess. Carefully submerge the fish in the oil and fry for about 4 minutes, then flip and fry the second side for 4 to 5 minutes. Use tongs to remove the fish from the oil and transfer it to paper towels to drain. Fry the remaining fish the same way. Serve with salsa verde.

SALSA VERDE

MAKES 2 CUPS

2 cloves garlic, peeled

2 cups tightly packed parsley leaves

1 tablespoon capers

¼ cup freshly squeezed lemon juice

1 tablespoon white wine vinegar

1 teaspoon salt

¼ teaspoon freshly ground pepper

⅔ cup extra-virgin olive oil

With the food processor motor running, drop in the garlic cloves and let them process until finely chopped. Turn off the motor and add the parsley, capers, lemon juice, vinegar, salt, and pepper. Pulse until the parsley is finely chopped, scraping down the sides as necessary. Turn the processor on and, with the motor running, drizzle in the olive oil. Pause to scrape down the sides and process until well combined. Taste and add more salt and lemon juice if desired. Keep tightly covered in the refrigerator until ready to serve.

Goat farming is on the rise in Cuba. The animal's meat not only provides farmers with a consistent form of income but is also a nutritious addition to the Cuban table. The government still controls around 90 percent of the farmland in Cuba, but as noted, they are giving away large swaths of "unarable" land—on which the ever-resourceful, cash-strapped Cubans are growing organic crops and raising healthy animals like goats, who thrive in environments unsuitable for most livestock varieties. This goat stew combines the Cubans' newfound love of goat meat with their abiding passion for slow-cooked one-pot meals. Start it cooking on a chilly winter's day, then snuggle up with a good book while the comforting aroma fills your home. It's especially hearty when ladled over a bowlful of rice but is also good on its own. It will store in the refrigerator for up to one week or in the freezer for months.

SAVORY GOAT STEW

SERVES 6 TO 8

2 pounds goat stew meat, trimmed and cut into 1½-inch cubes

⅓ cup freshly squeezed lime juice

6 cloves garlic, minced

1 tablespoon salt

3 tablespoons vegetable oil

1 large yellow onion, diced

1 large green bell pepper, stemmed, seeded, and diced

3 carrots, peeled and sliced into ½-inch-thick rounds

1 (28-ounce) can crushed tomatoes

3 Roma tomatoes, diced

1½ cups Chicken Stock (page 16)

2 teaspoons ground cumin

1 teaspoon dried oregano

Freshly ground pepper

White Rice (page 14), to serve

Chopped fresh cilantro, for garnish

Toss the goat meat with the lime juice, garlic, and salt in a mixing bowl. Cover and refrigerate for 1 hour.

Remove the meat from the marinade and pat it dry with paper towels, discarding the excess marinade. Heat the oil in a large Dutch oven or soup pot over high heat. When the oil is shimmering, brown the goat on all sides, about 4 to 6 minutes per side. Work in batches so as not to overcrowd the pan. Set the meat aside.

Lower the heat to medium-low. Working quickly so the browned bits in the pan don't start to burn, add the onion, pepper, and carrots to the pot. As the vegetables begin to sweat out some liquid, use a wooden spoon to scrape up the browned bits on the bottom of the pot. When the vegetables have softened, 8 to 10 minutes, add the meat back to the pot, along with the canned and fresh tomatoes, chicken stock, cumin, and oregano. Bring the stew to a boil, then lower the heat and simmer until the goat is fork-tender, 2 to 2½ hours. Season to taste with salt and pepper.

Serve the goat stew on top of white rice, garnished with the cilantro.

fincas

Raul Castro, Fidel's brother, who was elected president by Cuba's National Assembly in 2008, is slowly turning over millions of acres of land to the Cuban people. It is not an act of generosity; that land is deemed unsuitable for farming. However, industrious farmers, many of whom have waited a lifetime to own land of their own, are proving that ingenuity, creativity, and resourcefulness go a long way in transforming a patch of land deemed worthless into a flourishing farm—these are the *fincas* we described in our introduction. The *fincas* are being studied by farmers around the globe for their innovative agricultural practices. Instead of relying on expensive equipment, they emulate the traditions of past generations, who listened to the land and used what was around them to cultivate flourishing fields of abundance.

The Finca Agroecologica El Paraiso, in the heart of the Vinales Valley, is a paradise surrounded by iron-red *mogotes*, rounded mounds of land formed in the karstic environment—a landscape of insoluble rock that appears once the soluble rock around it has eroded. In Vinales, soft rock formations like dolomite, gypsum, and limestone are omnipresent. Vinales itself is designated a UNESCO World Heritage Site, and El Paraiso is its agricultural crown jewel.

It is here that the farmer Wilfredo, the family's patriarch, has transformed one of those patches of wasteland into a thriving farm that has become the national template for other *finca* owners to learn from and, more significantly, be inspired by. They revived the soil using a combination of legumes and alfalfa to infuse it with beneficial chemicals and minerals, and a healthy dose of patience to endure the years required to rekindle it. Today, Wilfredo and his hardworking family cultivate over sixty varieties of vegetables, fruits, and medicinal herbs—crops such

as mangoes, lemons, limes, tomatoes, cassava, mint, peas, potatoes, onions, garlic, and fennel, grown in raised beds to preserve the precious, fertile soil.

They use no chemical fertilizers, relying instead on time-tested techniques like nicotine fumigation, marigold borders, and sunflower oil insect traps. Their fertilizer comprises tobacco juice and rabbit manure, procured from a group of contented rabbits that feed on the farm's compost. Everything is recycled at El Paraiso, including the residual whey from their cheese and butter production, sold commercially as a healthful beverage and effective meat tenderizer.

The farm serves a bountiful lunch to the tourists and locals who flock to its open-air wooden patio overlooking the surrounding valley. Any leftover food (the meal is a feast of dizzying abundance) is donated to the local senior centers, military bases, and schools. Wilfredo and his family encourage school groups to take classes on the farm to teach children how to eventually cultivate similar farms of their own and to inspire in them an abiding sense of optimism. The farm offers a glimpse of these rare Cuban commodities and is rightfully embraced by farmers throughout the nation as a source of pride and promise.

Our lunch at El Paraiso seemed to include the farm's entire bounty. The women of the family lovingly prepared each dish in a breezy open-air kitchen toward the back of the house that they all share.

Congri was brought to the table along with goat cooked whole on a spit over mango wood kindled with corn husks. These dishes were accompanied by a soothing vegetable stew of corn, pumpkin, green beans, and potatoes. Turkey smoked over papaya wood was served alongside addicting malanga chips with a chorizo paste for slathering, a bowl of mashed yuca, and roasted bell peppers. The sea-saltiness of a robust hunk of bonito was tempered by an acidic tomato salsa, and a side of stewed red cabbage provided a pleasing counterpoint to the

condiment's vinegar kick. The meal was washed down with an "anti-stress" cocktail made with an abundance of medicinal herbs; guests could add a splash of local rum from the bottle placed with relish at the center of the table by Anna Maria, one of Wilfredo's enthusiastic daughters. Just when we thought we couldn't take another bite, a coconut flan of sweetened milk powder, sugar, lemon, vanilla, and a dash of cinnamon proved too tempting to pass up.

Following the feast, with a refreshing breeze from the valley below cooling our faces, our guide Reuben grabbed his stomach and announced it was time for a *sobra mesa*, which he described as something akin to a siesta at the table. We all agreed, poured ourselves one more shot of rum, and settled into a collective contented stupor, reflecting on the extraordinary glory of El Paraiso, a *finca* derived from nothing but a dream and an unwavering commitment to realizing it.

We enjoyed a snack of chicharrónes—pork skin fried until it's airy and light—on our way to Santa Maria Beach. They were being fried in a massive cast-iron pot hanging from a wooden tripod above a blazing fire. The pot was filled to the brim with bubbling oil stirred by a group of men using a wooden ladle as tall as they were. Chicharrónes are traditionally made of pork skin that is sold in markets throughout the Americas, Mexico, and the Caribbean in large segments the size and shape of elephant ears. In Cuba, the oil of choice is sunflower, but in this recipe, we've lightened it up and omitted the oil (and the skin) altogether. Instead, chunks of pork shoulder are first marinated in a juice combination, then slow-cooked for hours, which leaves them crispy and infused with tropical flavor. They're fantastic with mojitos or a pitcher of beer. Just be sure to make a large batch—they tend to go fast.

ISLAND-STYLE CHICHAR-RÓNES

SERVES 8 TO 10 AS AN
APPETIZER OR SNACK

½ cup dark brown sugar

5 cloves garlic, minced

5 teaspoons salt

2½ teaspoons cayenne pepper

2 teaspoons ground cumin

2 teaspoons smoked paprika

2 teaspoons dried oregano

2 pounds boneless pork shoulder, cut into 2-inch cubes, fat left intact

½ cup canned or bottled mango nectar

½ cup unsweetened coconut milk

¼ cup freshly squeezed lime juice

Mix together the brown sugar, garlic, salt, cayenne, cumin, paprika, and oregano in a small bowl.

Place the pork in a large ziplock bag, add about half of the spice mix, and seal the bag. Squeeze the pork around inside the bag so it gets coated with the rub. Open the bag and pour in the mango nectar, coconut milk, and lime juice. Reseal the bag and again squeeze and massage it to make sure everything is well combined. Place the bag in the refrigerator for at least 2 hours and up to overnight, turning several times to redistribute the marinade.

Pour the contents of the bag into a colander to drain off the excess liquid, then transfer the pork to a large skillet. Add enough water to cover the pork, 1 to 1½ cups. Place the skillet over low heat and cook uncovered for 3½ to 4 hours, stirring gently every 30 minutes, until all the water has cooked off and the pork is brown and crispy. Drain the chicharrónes on paper towels, sprinkle with the remaining spice mix, and serve hot.

Fried chicken is a crowd favorite throughout Cuba, and we ate, or rather devoured, our favorite in the Vinales region following an afternoon of learning how to roll cigars in a drying house nearby. The version in this recipe is marinated for several hours in sour (or bitter) orange juice, then battered with a layer of buttermilk that helps tenderize it and imparts a subtle tanginess. It's fantastic when served piping hot fresh from the fryer and also wonderful cold, making it an ideal recipe to arrange a picnic around.

CUBAN FRIED CHICKEN

SERVES 6 TO 8

2 (3-pound) fryer chickens, each cut into 8 pieces

6 cloves garlic, smashed with the side of a knife

1 cup bottled sour orange juice, or ⅔ cup freshly squeezed orange juice mixed with ⅜ cup freshly squeezed lime juice

1 teaspoon ground cumin

2 tablespoons salt, divided

½ teaspoon freshly ground pepper

3 cups all-purpose flour

1 teaspoon garlic powder

1 teaspoon dried oregano

1 teaspoon smoked paprika

2 cups buttermilk

Vegetable oil for deep-frying

Arrange the chicken in a large glass baking dish. Whisk together the garlic cloves, sour orange juice, cumin, 1 tablespoon of the salt, and the pepper in a small bowl. Pour this mixture over the chicken and cover the dish with plastic wrap. Refrigerate for at least 4 hours and up to 24 hours, turning the chicken at least once.

Whisk together the flour, garlic powder, oregano, paprika, and remaining 1 tablespoon salt in a large bowl. Divide the seasoned flour between two shallow baking dishes or pie pans. Pour the buttermilk into a third dish or pie pan. To set up your breading station, place the pan of buttermilk between the two pans of seasoned flour and line a large baking sheet with parchment paper or aluminum foil.

Heat at least 4 inches of oil to 350°F in a large, heavy pot over medium-high heat. The oil should be deep enough to completely submerge several pieces of chicken. Remove the chicken from the marinade and discard the excess marinade. Dredge the chicken in the first pan of seasoned flour, then dip it in the buttermilk. Remove the chicken from the buttermilk pan, allowing the excess buttermilk to drip off, and roll it in the second pan of seasoned flour. As you are breading, try to use one hand for wet work and one hand for dry to minimize the mess. Place the coated chicken on the prepared baking sheet.

Working in batches of 3 or 4 pieces of chicken at a time, lower the chicken into the hot oil and fry until dark golden, turning the pieces periodically to ensure even browning. Use a meat thermometer to check for doneness; the temperature should register at least 165°F. When done, remove from the oil and drain on a rack set over a baking sheet. Sprinkle the hot chicken with salt and pepper.

We're dubious that *frituras de maiz*, or corn fritters, are really the precursor to Fritos, but we are sure that we will always prefer these airy corn fritters to a bag of greasy chips. We tried our first *frituras de maiz* after visiting a fruit market in Vinales. They were being fried to order by a woman wearing a rainbow-striped halter top straight out of a 1970s skating rink. She scooped a spoonful into a newspaper cone, sprinkled them with salt, added a side of sweet-and-sour dipping sauce, and with an enormous grin handed them over to us. We were instantly hooked. The version we offer here is gussied up a bit with the addition of bell pepper, fresh corn, parsley, and onion. Tip: If you invert a small bowl in a much larger bowl and place your ear of corn on top of the smaller bowl's underside, you can cut all the way to the bottom of the cob without damaging your knife or creating a mess, since the larger bowl will collect the kernels as they spill off.

FRITURAS DE MAIZ (FRIED CORNMEAL)

SERVES 6 TO 8 AS
AN APPETIZER

2 cups fresh corn kernels, cut from about 4 ears of corn, divided

½ cup medium-coarse cornmeal

½ yellow onion, coarsely chopped

1 egg

1 tablespoon sugar

1 teaspoon salt

½ teaspoon freshly ground pepper

½ cup all-purpose flour

½ red bell pepper, stemmed, seeded, and minced

2 tablespoons chopped fresh parsley

Vegetable oil for deep-frying

Combine 1½ cups of the corn kernels with the cornmeal, onion, egg, sugar, salt, and pepper in a food processor. Pulse to just blend the ingredients. The batter should still be slightly chunky. Pour the mixture into a mixing bowl and stir in the remaining ½ cup corn kernels, flour, red pepper, and parsley.

Heat at least 4 inches of oil in a large, heavy pot over medium-high heat until the oil temperature reaches 375°F. Gently drop the batter by tablespoonfuls into the hot oil, being sure not to overcrowd the pan, as this will lower the oil temperature and cause your fritters to soak up oil like little sponges. Not appetizing! Fry for about 5 minutes, until cooked through. Sprinkle the fritters with a little extra salt and serve hot.

Lamb is not as common as pork or chicken in Cuba, but we did see a few sheep farms on the three-hour drive from Havana to Vinales. It's a favored ingredient for stews and other one-pot meals, served with a big plate of rice to sop up all the juices. This is our twist on that island favorite, but instead of making a stew, we've fried shredded lamb to achieve a caramelized flavor. It's delicious served with a fresh tomato salad, making this an ideal recipe for late summer when tomatoes are succulent and luscious.

CRISPY TWICE-COOKED LAMB

SERVES 4

1 whole (3-pound) lamb shoulder

1 yellow onion, peeled and halved

1 green bell pepper, stemmed, halved, and seeded

1 head garlic, unpeeled and halved horizontally

2 bay leaves

1 tablespoon plus 1 teaspoon salt, divided

½ cup bottled sour orange juice, or ⅓ cup freshly squeezed orange juice mixed with 3 tablespoons freshly squeezed lime juice

4 cloves garlic, minced

About 5 tablespoons vegetable oil, as needed

2 cups thinly sliced yellow onion

White Rice (page 14)

Place the lamb in a large, heavy pot with the halved onion, bell pepper, garlic, the bay leaves, and the 1 tablespoon of salt. Add enough water to cover the lamb by about 3 inches. Bring to a boil, then lower the heat and simmer until the lamb is fork-tender, 2 to 3 hours.

Lift the lamb out of the braising liquid and set it aside to cool. Strain the liquid through a fine-mesh sieve, discarding the vegetables, and save it for another use (having frozen lamb stock on hand is fantastic when you want to make a lamb stew).

When the lamb is cool enough to handle, shred the meat into strips with your hands, keeping longer pieces together if possible. As you shred, scrape off any excess fat and discard.

In a medium bowl, mix the cleaned and shredded lamb, sour orange juice, minced garlic, and the remaining teaspoon of salt. Let the meat marinate for at least 1 hour in the refrigerator, or up to 4 hours.

Heat 2 tablespoons of the oil in a large, heavy skillet, preferably cast iron. Remove the meat from the marinade and squeeze out the excess liquid with your hands. When the oil is shimmering, add the lamb and cook for about 10 minutes, stirring and scraping the pan occasionally, until the lamb is browned and crisp. You may need to work in batches to avoid overcrowding the pan. With each new batch, add a little fresh oil.

When all of the lamb has been crisped, add 1 more tablespoon of vegetable oil to the skillet and cook the onion until soft, scraping up any browned bits from the bottom of the pan as you go. Return the lamb to the pan and stir everything together. Serve with lots of white rice.

Along the road to Viñales, every few miles we saw vendors stationed on the roadside with trays of fresh white farmer's cheese, buns, and plastic bags filled with guava paste. "¡Pan con timba!" our guide Reuben yelled when he spotted the first vendor. "What?" we asked. He explained that when the Americans lived in Cuba in the last century, they used to carry their guava paste in wooden boxes, hence the name "bread with wood" for this winning combination. This recipe is our incarnation of it. Instead of buns, we've stuffed easy-to-execute hand pies with cream cheese and guava paste (see page 116), creating a portable snack for young and old alike.

GUAVA HAND PIES

SERVES 4 TO 6

2½ cups all-purpose flour

1 tablespoon sugar

1 teaspoon salt

1 cup (2 sticks) cold unsalted butter, cut into small cubes

About 3 tablespoons ice-cold water

8 ounces guava paste

8 ounces cream cheese, chilled

1 egg

Whisk together the flour, sugar, and salt in a large bowl. Add the butter and use a pastry blender or your fingers to work it into the flour until it looks like coarse meal, with no butter chunks bigger than a pea. You should be able to form clumps by squeezing a chunk of dough in your hand. Add the water, 1 tablespoon at a time, and mix with your hands or a rubber spatula until the dough comes together. Divide the dough into two chunks and flatten each chunk into a disk. Wrap each disk in plastic wrap and refrigerate for at least 1 hour.

Roll out one disk of dough to about ¼ inch thick on a well-floured board, shooting for a 6 by 12-inch rectangle. Cut the rectangle into eight 3-inch squares. Line a baking sheet with parchment paper. Carefully transfer the squares to the baking sheet and cover with plastic wrap. Place the sheet in the refrigerator while you roll out and cut the second disk of dough in the same manner, giving you 16 squares of dough.

Slice the guava paste into ¼-inch-thick pieces roughly 2 inches by 2 inches. Slice the cream cheese in the same way.

Beat the egg with 1 tablespoon of water. Working with 8 squares of pastry dough, place a slice of guava paste and a slice of cream cheese in the center of each square. Using a pastry brush, brush the egg wash around the edge of each square, then top with another pastry square and seal each parcel tightly, crimping the edges with a fork. Transfer the assembled pies to the parchment-lined baking sheet and place them in the freezer for 1 hour.

Preheat the oven to 425°F. Brush the frozen pies all over with egg wash and bake for 10 minutes, then lower the heat to 350°F and bake for another 30 minutes, until the pies are golden brown. Let the pies cool slightly before serving, or serve at room temperature.

azucar (sugar)

Without the black market in Cuba there would be little on the table but basics assembled from meager government rations. This underground system keeps the economy moving, padding paltry earnings with an extra dose of revenue. For many resourceful Cubans, income from the products and services they sell carries them from one month to the next. The black market also keeps Cuban cuisine dynamic and interesting.

Everyone depends on the black market, from restaurant owners to government officials. If you're caught buying or selling within the underground system, you will go to trial, and the punishment can be severe. However, most people don't get caught, because in practice authorities tend to look the other way, since even police officers and military brass rely on it. Our friend Reuben affirmed this: "Even Fidel Castro must buy from the black market; there is no other way to survive in this country." Reuben spent an entire afternoon trying to explain to us how he once sold cable on the black market because even access to television channels, movies, and the Internet depends on this complex and vital system. "Once you find the right person, you stick with them," Reuben explained. His favorite black market ingredients included lobster, chocolate, fish, rum, and the occasional cigar.

Cuban desserts are one of the prime dependents on the black market system. Without it, there wouldn't be much to concoct a confection with other than sugar, salt, and flour.

We visited a black market bakery where the owner employed six bakers who produced an astonishing array of Cuban sweets—like pastelitos, churros, bunuelos, and turrones—in the back of a socialized living arrangement where the families shared everything, including the tantalizing aroma of pastries fresh from the oven.

The bakers worked at breakneck speed, transferring sheet trays filled with dozens of goodies from oven to speed rack with adept precision. Beyond the professional, many-tiered speed racks, their equipment was meager: dented metal bowls, an assortment of battered spatulas, a tarnished whisk or two, an industrial-sized mixer that worked only intermittently, and a few other odds and ends served a bakery that each day produced hundreds of confections that would rival those of the world's most esteemed pastry shops.

The owner, who asked us not to use his name for fear of discovery, told us he had been in business for six years, and in that time fundamental equipment such as their mixer and ovens broke down continuously. He reassured us, though, that he never feared losing one permanently. "Look at how long we have kept our cars going. If we can do that with a Ford from the 1960s, we can manage to repair a mixer without a problem. It's in our blood."

In the Plaza Vieja, Havana's Old Square, there are a number of nationalized pastry shops, but none felt as genuine as the one we visited

hidden behind an imposing wooden door on a random side street in a hard-to-find corner of the city. We suspect the owner likes it this way, preserving his secret location not to avoid notoriety but to keep himself in business, and also to avoid landing in prison. The hundreds of Cubans who indulge in his team's creations, purchased from metal bicycle baskets, hope that he's never discovered either. His secret is safe with us.

guava & coconut pastilles

On the outskirts of Havana, a few miles from the house where Ernest Hemingway wrote some of his most beloved classics, including *The Old Man and the Sea*, we visited a black market pastry shed located in the back of a house and comprising little more than one metal work bench, a single-basin sink, and an industrial-sized oven.

Here brothers Darien and Michael produced, each work day, two thousand buttery, flaky pastilles stuffed with guava paste or coconut paste. Their baking skills would have earned them prime positions in the finest Parisian bakery, but instead they were toiling away from sunrise to dusk, baking a small portion of Havana's black market pastries that are collected each day by bicycle vendors and sold for the equivalent of a few cents to those with a sweet tooth throughout the city.

Fruit is a primary component in many Cuban pastries, its quality and variety contingent on whether or not the market is nationalized or privatized. At the nationalized markets, there is standard fare, such as papayas, mangoes, guavas, and coconuts, but there is much more at the private, free-enterprise markets, where more unusual fruits from the countryside—such as the one variously called cherimoya, guanabana, or soursop—are waiting to be discovered.

Churros are a cherished comfort dessert throughout much of the Americas, Mexico, and the Caribbean, and Cuba is no exception. We saw them everywhere on the streets of Havana. They are sold from tiny, festively decorated street carts, no bigger than a post office box but painted bright colors to entice the churro aficionado in all of us. Churros are inexpensive and fun to handle in all their elongated star-shaped glory. When properly fried, they have a crisp exterior that easily gives way to a piping hot center of airy pleasure. Sprinkle them with cinnamon sugar when still piping hot, and get them to the table as lickety-split as you can possibly manage.

CHURROS

SERVES 6 TO 8

1 cup plus 2 tablespoons sugar, divided
2 teaspoons ground cinnamon
1 cup water
¼ cup (½ stick) butter
½ teaspoon salt
1 cup all-purpose flour
4 eggs
Vegetable oil for deep-frying

Mix 1 cup of the sugar with the cinnamon in a large bowl and set aside.

Combine the remaining 2 tablespoons of sugar with the water, butter, and salt in a saucepan and bring the mixture just to a boil. Add the flour all at once and stir vigorously until the dough pulls away from the sides of the pan, 1 to 2 minutes. Remove the pan from the heat and transfer the mixture to a mixing bowl or the bowl of a stand mixer. Add the eggs one at a time, either stirring by hand or beating on low speed until each one is incorporated before adding the next. Note that adding the eggs will seem to break the dough, but it will eventually come back together as you continue mixing. Transfer the mixture into a pastry bag fitted with a star tip.

Heat at least 4 inches of oil in a heavy pot over medium-high heat until it reaches 350°F. Working in small batches, pipe 4- to 5-inch lengths of dough into the hot oil, using a small knife to carefully cut the dough to length. Fry until the churros are browned and cooked in the center, 4 to 5 minutes (cut open the first churro to test for doneness).

Remove the churros from the oil using a spider or slotted spoon. Drain on paper towels, and toss with the cinnamon sugar to coat. Serve warm or at room temperature.

Flan is the custard dessert that makes the whole world sing, and it's a particular favorite in Cuba. In this incarnation, the addition of pumpkin puree and autumn-scented spices like cinnamon, ginger, and nutmeg make this a prime dessert for your harvest table. Flan is mostly prepared on the black market in Cuba (see page 211), but we think even Fidel Castro would agree that it's well worth the risk that its producers take to sell it. The one challenge in this recipe is the caramel, an ingredient whose preparation seems to intimidate even the most skilled cooks. Do not fret. If you follow the instructions step by step, we guarantee that your caramel will not fail you. Your flan (and your guests) will thank you for it.

PUMPKIN FLAN

SERVES 8 TO 10

⅓ cup plus ¼ cup sugar, divided
2 tablespoons water
5 eggs
1 teaspoon pure vanilla extract
½ teaspoon ground cinnamon
¼ teaspoon ground ginger
¼ teaspoon ground nutmeg
1 cup pumpkin puree
1 (14-ounce) can sweetened condensed milk
1 (12-ounce) can evaporated milk
1 cup whole milk

Preheat the oven to 350°F. Combine the ⅓ cup sugar and the water in a small saucepan over medium heat. Heat without stirring until the sugar begins to turn golden around the edges of the pan. Gently swirl the pan rather than stirring it until all of the sugar turns to amber-colored caramel. Pour the caramel into a 9 by 5-inch loaf pan and tip the pan to coat the entire bottom evenly. Set the pan aside.

Whisk together the eggs and the remaining ¼ cup sugar until combined. Stir in the vanilla, cinnamon, ginger, nutmeg, and pumpkin.

Add the three milks and continue stirring until the mixture is smooth and homogenous. Pour the custard over the caramel in the loaf pan.

Set the filled loaf pan inside a 9 by 13-inch baking pan. Pour hot water into the outer pan until it comes halfway up the sides of the loaf pan. Bake until the flan is nearly set in the middle, 1½ to 2 hours. Cover the flan and refrigerate it for at least 8 hours or overnight.

Run a knife around the edge of the chilled flan and invert the loaf pan onto an appropriately sized platter. Slice the flan and serve.

azucar (sugar)

This is such a beautiful cake to bring with you to a gathering where something festive but light is the order of the day. Tres leches refers to this cake's trinity of coconut, evaporated, and sweetened condensed milks, and as we learned both in Cuba and at home in our kitchen when testing this recipe, this method will never fail you. With toasted coconut and sliced mango added just before serving, this cake sings "¡Cuba!" to us with every delectable bite.

COCONUT TRES LECHES CAKE

SERVES 10 TO 12

1½ cups flour

1 teaspoon baking powder

1½ teaspoons salt

½ cup (1 stick) unsalted butter, at room temperature

1 cup sugar

1 teaspoon pure vanilla extract

5 eggs, at room temperature

1 (14-ounce) can coconut milk

1 (12-ounce) can evaporated milk

1 (14-ounce) can sweetened condensed milk

1 cup unsweetened coconut flakes, toasted

1 large mango, peeled and diced

Preheat the oven to 350°F. Grease a 9 by 13-inch cake pan or baking dish.

Whisk together the flour, baking powder, and salt in a mixing bowl. Set aside.

Using an electric mixer, cream the butter, sugar, and vanilla until fluffy. Add one egg at a time until all of the eggs are incorporated. Fold in the dry mixture. Pour the batter into the prepared pan and bake for 30 minutes, or until a toothpick inserted into the middle of the cake comes out clean. Allow the cake to cool slightly in the pan, about 10 minutes.

While the cake is cooling, whisk together the coconut milk, evaporated milk, and sweetened condensed milk. Use a toothpick or wooden skewer to poke the cake, making many, many tiny holes all over. Slowly pour the milk mixture evenly over the top of the cake. Cover and refrigerate for at least 5 hours and up to 1 day.

Garnish the cake with the toasted coconut and mango, slice, and serve.

RICE PUDDING

Arroz con leche, or rice pudding, is beloved throughout Cuba. It's a festive finish to any meal, and it's a dessert that doesn't drain the wallet—which cash-strapped Cubans who refuse to quell their passion for the good life sincerely appreciate. In this recipe, it's garnished with toasted coconut, a flourish that adds even more panache to this irresistible sweet. Note that the pudding will thicken substantially as it cools, so plan to remove it from the stove when it's thinner than you prefer. If you keep cooking it past the point of just thickening on the heat, you run the risk of the pudding seizing up like a brick. With practice, you'll get to know just the right point at which to stop cooking.

RICE PUDDING
WITH TOASTED COCONUT

SERVES 6 TO 8

½ cup Valencia
(or any short-grain) rice

1½ cups water

3 tablespoons sugar

3 cups whole milk

1 (14-ounce) can sweetened condensed milk

½ teaspoon salt

1 cinnamon stick

1 vanilla bean, split, or
1 teaspoon pure vanilla extract

1 long strip lemon peel, yellow part only (As much as you can get in one go—peeling around the lemon at a slight angle with a vegetable peeler works well.)

½ cup sweetened shredded coconut, toasted

Ground cinnamon, for sprinkling

Put the rice and water in a medium saucepan and bring to a boil. Boil uncovered until all the water is absorbed, 7 to 10 minutes, then turn off the heat.

Meanwhile, stir together the sugar, whole milk, condensed milk, and salt in a mixing bowl. Add the milk mixture to the rice and return the pot to medium heat. Stir to make sure no rice is stuck to the bottom. Stir in the cinnamon stick, vanilla bean, and lemon peel. Cook the mixture for 30 to 40 minutes, until the pudding just starts to thicken, stirring often.

Fish out the lemon peel, cinnamon stick, and vanilla bean. Pour the pudding into a glass baking dish and cover with plastic wrap. Chill the pudding until it is fully set. Top with toasted coconut and a sprinkle of ground cinnamon.

Havana's Coppelia is one of the largest ice cream parlors in the world. It's reminiscent of an aquarium, with aquamarine-painted walls that undulate like ocean waves throughout two levels. Cubans line up for hours to savor a cone topped with one of the flavors of the day.

CARA-MELIZED GRILLED PINEAPPLE
WITH TOASTED COCONUT ICE CREAM

SERVES 6 TO 8

1 large fresh pineapple
½ cup brown sugar
½ stick butter
2 tablespoons dark rum
1 teaspoon salt
Toasted Coconut Ice Cream (see recipe), for serving

Cut the top and bottom off of the pineapple and then cut off the skin, removing as little fruit as possible. Cut the whole pineapple in half, then in quarters. Remove the core from each quarter and slice each quarter crosswise into 1-inch-thick slices. Toss the pineapple slices with the brown sugar and set aside.

Prepare a medium-high-heat grill. First clean the grates thoroughly and brush or wipe them with oil.

While the grill heats, melt the butter in a small saucepan and stir in the rum and salt. When the grill is ready, lay the pineapple slices directly on the grates and brush them generously with the rum butter. Grill until the slices are golden brown, then flip and brush them with more rum butter.

TOASTED COCONUT ICE CREAM

MAKES ABOUT 2 QUARTS

2 cups sweetened coconut flakes
3 cups half-and-half
3 cups coconut milk (unsweetened)
8 egg yolks
1 cup sugar
1 teaspoon salt
1 teaspoon vanilla

Preheat the oven to 325°F. Spread out the coconut in a single layer on a rimmed baking sheet and toast in the oven for about 10 minutes, until the flakes turn golden brown at the tips, checking often.

Stir together the half-and-half, coconut milk, and toasted coconut in a large saucepan and bring to a boil. Remove the mixture from the heat and let it stand for 30 minutes.

Meanwhile, whisk together the egg yolks, sugar, salt, and vanilla until thick and well combined. Strain the coconut milk mixture into a clean pot and bring it to a simmer. Temper the egg yolk mixture by whisking in a small amount of the hot liquid to warm it up, then add all of the egg mixture to the hot liquid, whisking constantly.

Place the custard over medium-low heat and cook, stirring, until it thickens, 8 to 10 minutes. Strain through a fine-mesh sieve and immediately cool in an ice bath.

Process in a standard ice cream machine.

Flan and coffee are two edibles that it seems all Cubans crave. This recipe brings them together in a highly pleasurable way. A slice of this flan is a nice way to close a meal, and it's also wonderful in the morning when you need a little extra boost to get you going. Of course, do as the Cubans do, and be sure you wash it down with a strong cup of café con leche.

CUBAN COFFEE FLAN

SERVES 8 TO 10

⅔ cup sugar, divided
2 tablespoons water
3 cups half-and-half
⅓ cup espresso-grind coffee
6 eggs
½ teaspoon vanilla extract
½ teaspoon salt
1 (14-ounce) can sweetened condensed milk

Preheat the oven to 350°F. Heat ⅓ cup of the sugar and the water in a small, heavy saucepan over medium heat until the sugar around the edges of the pan begins to turn golden. Rather than stirring, swirl the pan to evenly caramelize the sugar to an amber color. Remove the pan from the heat and pour the caramel evenly into a 9 by 5-inch loaf pan, tilting the pan to coat the entire bottom. Set aside.

Heat the half-and-half in a saucepan until barely simmering. Remove the pan from the heat, stir in the coffee, then cover and steep for 5 minutes.

Beat together the eggs, remaining ⅓ cup sugar, vanilla, and salt in a large bowl. Strain the coffee-infused half-and-half through a fine-mesh sieve twice to remove all of the coffee grounds. Add the coffee mixture to the egg mixture, whisking constantly. Stir in the condensed milk.

Pour the custard mixture into the loaf pan. Set the filled loaf pan inside a 9 by 13-inch baking pan and pour hot water into the outer pan until it comes halfway up the sides of the loaf pan. Place the pan in the oven and bake until the custard is almost set in the middle, 1½ to 2 hours.

Remove the loaf pan from the baking dish and let it cool on a rack until it is cool enough to place in the refrigerator. Chill for at least 4 hours.

Unmold the flan by running a sharp knife around the edges and inverting it onto a platter. Slice and serve.

black market flan

Raul Perez Cordero is a celebrated Cuban abstract painter whose work adorns many of Havana's most illustrious galleries, but among Havana's culinary insiders, his mother Juana is more famous than her talented son.

She is a black market flan producer who lives in a diminutive apartment toward the back of a series of seemingly endless corridors lined with doors that lead to who knows what other black market producers. Her turquoise blue walls are adorned from floor to ceiling with her son's contemporary, fantastical artwork, of which she is clearly and justifiably proud.

When we arrived, Juana was in the midst of unmolding a large flan; she hardens her creations in gallon-sized, recycled aluminum tins. This soft-spoken elderly woman with gray hair and a gentle smile made us feel right at home.

Juana first told us proudly in Spanish that she has six sons, but then her voice sank as she explained that she had lost one. The lilt in her voice returned when she explained how she first became involved in the black market flan-making business.

"The restaurant Garden of Eden used to request a flan or two from me every week, but then they started asking for more, and soon the word spread that I made some of the best flans in the city. Restaurants all over town started requesting them, and I used to stay awake until 2 a.m. each night making flans." She began slicing her velvety flan into generous triangles. "I'm too old for that now, but I still bake about one dozen flans a day. During low season I make between eight and ten, and during high season it's sometimes between seventeen and twenty. It's hard work, but I enjoy it. My flan is what got my family through some very difficult times, and I will always be grateful for the doors it opened for my sons."

With that, Juana distributed her flan onto vintage plates with a Victorian motif and drizzled each slice with a ribbon of chestnut-hued caramel. We protested that the slices were too generous, but she waved her hands. "Nonsense. You can never have too much flan."

MOJITO CAKE WITH RUM-INFUSED WHIPPED CREAM AND LIME ZEST

SERVES 10 TO 12

CAKE

3 cups all-purpose flour

3 teaspoons baking powder

1 teaspoon salt

1 cup (2 sticks) unsalted butter, at room temperature

2 cups sugar

4 eggs, at room temperature

2 teaspoons pure vanilla extract

2 teaspoons lime zest

1 teaspoon rum extract

2 tablespoons freshly squeezed lime juice

½ cup whole milk

LIME-MINT SYRUP

¼ cup water

¼ cup brown sugar

¼ cup packed fresh mint leaves

¼ cup freshly squeezed lime juice

WHIPPED CREAM

2 cups heavy cream, chilled

2 tablespoons powdered sugar

1 tablespoon dark rum

Lime slices, or 1 teaspoon lime zest, for topping

Preheat the oven to 350°F. Grease two 9-inch round cake pans and line the bottoms with parchment paper.

To make the cake, whisk together the flour, baking powder, and salt in a mixing bowl and set aside.

Using a stand mixer or an electric hand mixer, beat together the butter and sugar until light and fluffy, 5 to 7 minutes. Beat in the eggs one at a time, making sure each egg is fully incorporated before adding the next. Stir in the vanilla, lime zest, rum extract, and lime juice. Fold in the dry ingredients until just combined. Add the milk and stir until smooth.

Divide the batter evenly between the two prepared cake pans and bake for 30 to 40 minutes, until the cake springs back at a touch and starts to slightly pull away from the sides. Remove from the oven and set the pans on a rack to cool. After 10 minutes, remove the cakes from the pans and let them cool completely on the rack.

While the cakes are cooling, make the syrup. Heat the water and brown sugar in a small saucepan over medium heat, stirring until all of the sugar is dissolved. Stir in the mint leaves, cover, and set aside for 10 minutes to steep. After 10 minutes, strain out the mint leaves and stir in the lime juice. Set aside.

To make the whipped cream, place either a large metal mixing bowl or the metal bowl of a stand mixer in the refrigerator until well chilled. Pour the cold cream into the chilled bowl and begin beating it, using either an electric hand mixer or the whip attachment of the stand mixer. When the cream has partially thickened, sprinkle in the powdered sugar and continue beating. When the whipped cream holds stiff peaks, stir in the rum.

If your cakes are very domed, use a slicing knife to trim the tops of the cakes so they are flat. Using a pastry brush, liberally brush the top of each cake with the syrup. Place the first cake on a plate, bottom side up, and spoon half the whipped cream onto the center. Using an offset or regular spatula, push the whipped cream out toward the edges of the cake, without going all the way to the edge. The weight of the second layer will push it the rest of the way. Center the second layer on top of the first, bottom side down, and press down gently to push the whipped cream out slightly. Top with the remaining whipped cream and sprinkle with the lime zest. Either serve or chill immediately.

If you seek a festive dessert that your guests have most likely never enjoyed before, you've come to the right place. This recipe delivers the mojito in myriad ways, first in its batter, then in its whipped cream, and finally with a drizzle of lime-mint syrup that ensures its memory will linger long after the last hint of mint has faded from the palate. To add an even more momentous finish to this recipe (which we hope will become the culmination of at least one of your backyard barbecues this summer), the cake is layered, each portion delivering another piece of Cuban heaven. It's a dish you will remember, right down to your last rum-soaked bite.

Crispy fried dough with wine! Has anything ever sounded more alluring to the glutton in all of us? Chiviricos are a classic Cuban snack that are as tasty as they are addictively poppable. They are sold like potato chips in individual-sized bags throughout Havana, but they're oh so much better fresh. Serve them piping hot with a dusting of cinnamon sugar accompanied by pitchers of beer, and you've got a surefire hit on your hands.

CHIVIRICOS

SERVES 8 TO 10 AS A SNACK OR A SWEET EXTRA ON THE DESSERT TABLE

1 cup all-purpose flour

1 cup plus 1 tablespoon sugar, divided

½ teaspoon salt

1 egg

2 tablespoons white wine

4 tablespoons vegetable oil, plus more for deep-frying

2 teaspoons ground cinnamon

Whisk together the flour, 1 tablespoon of the sugar, and the salt in a medium bowl. Make a small well in the center of the dry mixture and add the egg, wine, and oil. Mix the wet into the dry with your fingers, adding just enough cold water to bring the dough together. Knead the dough a few times on a clean surface to make sure everything is combined, then flatten it into a disk and wrap it in plastic wrap. Refrigerate the dough for at least 1 hour.

Whisk together the remaining 1 cup of sugar and the cinnamon in a small bowl. Heat at least 4 inches of vegetable oil to 375°F in a heavy pot set over medium-high heat.

Remove the dough from the refrigerator. Tear off a grape-sized piece with your fingers and use a rolling pin to flatten it on a floured surface until it is as thin as possible. Paper-thin is the goal. You can slice the flattened dough into strips or leave the piece whole.

Drop the dough into the hot oil and fry until it is golden brown and very crispy. Remove the crisp dough from the oil using a spider or slotted spoon and drain on paper towels. While still warm, sprinkle with the cinnamon sugar.

Believe it or not, there's more to Cuban beverages than the beloved cocktails whose popularity has spread like the syrup of muddled mint leaf throughout the world.

First, there is beer, which is brewed in large, government-owned breweries throughout the nation. The two most renowned brands are Cristal, a basic lager served in a green, red, and white can, and Bucanero, a more complex brew with a deeper, more nuanced flavor. Both beers are brewed by the same large corporation, but in recent years smaller microbreweries have emerged. Most are still run by the government, and their brews are difficult to locate, but there is hope that with the advent of a more independent way of operating within the food and beverage system in Cuba there will emerge independently owned breweries crafting microbrews in small batches that reflect the terroir of the Cuban landscape.

Coffee is another beverage beloved by the Cuban people. Like so many other resources throughout the nation, such as sugarcane and cacao beans, most of the coffee beans produced there are exported by the government to other parts of the world, leaving the Cuban people scrambling for a fair share of their own natural resources.

But there has always been just enough coffee available to keep Cuba's people buzzing on a darkly roasted, robust elixir that jump starts each day, cutting through the fog that lingers from the rum-smoked festivities of the previous evening.

Throughout Havana, small cafes are popping up that proudly roast their own beans, a step once done only at the larger coffee roasters. This newfound attention to detail creates a more refined coffee culture that Cubans are coming to expect and encourage.

Juice is another mainstay in the Cuban beverage repertoire. We visited one of Havana's only independently owned juice shops, called a *jugero*, serving a whopping eighty-five varieties of freshly squeezed juices. There were the expected varieties, like papaya, mango, lime, and guava, but also more interesting concoctions, like a tamarind juice laced with lime, salt, and a hint of chile.

We were not surprised to find coffee, beer, and juice as beverages of choice in Cuba, but pru was another story. We first discovered this effervescent homemade beverage while exploring a fruit market with our guide, Reuben. He stopped in his tracks when he saw the pru vendor and insisted on buying some for us, paying with the local pesos that are illegal for tourists to possess. "Try this; it's the drink of the

with a t

people." We couldn't resist that endorsement. Its flavor was funky and earthy and virtually impossible to identify. Reuben explained that pru is made by fermenting roots in the sun, essentially making a fermented root iced tea.

But even the unique flavor of pru is no competition for Cuba's official beverage of choice: rum. Rum forms the foundation of virtually every classic Cuban cocktail, of which there are many. The Bacardi family fled Cuba following the Revolution, leaving only their distillery behind. Today it has been turned into a museum offering tours that tourists flock to for a symbolic reminder of yet another facet of Cuban history lost in the wake of the Revolution.

Bacardi may have closed its doors, but Havana Club endured, easily slipping into the nation's number one rum brand slot. Cuba takes its cocktails seriously, and all bartenders are judged by the standards of the Cuban Bartenders Association, a respected organization that traces its mysterious origins back to the Freemasons and is one of the few private organizations that the government still allows to operate openly.

One evening, we followed Reuben up a narrow flight of stairs in Old Havana to an apartment door where we were greeted by Julio and his wife, Rosio. We soon learned, after stepping into Julio's apartment with its floor-to-ceiling shelves overflowing with rum bottles, that he is the president of the Bartenders Association, and we would be making cocktails with the master.

One-third of the family's sprawling apartment has been converted into a bar in which the bartender shakes and muddles his way to cocktail perfection. He also consults for Havana Club, but of all his libation-related achievements, he seemed to be the most proud of his daughter, a celebrated bartender in her own right who until very recently was head bartender at the most famous of Ernest Hemingway's Cuban haunts, El Floridita.

Julio grew up in the cocktail business, learning the trade from a grandfather who owned a bar that the grandkids grew up in; Julio could craft the perfect cocktail before he was ten. The art is in his blood, and as he poured cocktail after cocktail for us, he confided that the Cubanito was his favorite due to its balance of sweet and acidic. He told us that the three essential ingredients for a foolproof Cuban cocktail are good limes, high-quality rum, and well-balanced simple syrup.

After a few more cocktails (we seemed to be drinking our way through the entire Cuban repertoire that evening), he told us, "The best advice I ever received to be a good bartender was to be elegant, be righteous, be respectful. You must have the ability to talk about anything, you should never judge anyone, and you should always be polite." Handing each of us a Cuba Libre, he continued, "The relationship between the barman and the client is the ultimate bond, but you also need to know how to keep your distance. Love your profession and never stop being creative."

papa hemingway

We visited Ernest Hemingway's home, Finca la Vigia (Lookout House), on a sunny but breezy morning, ideal for making this requisite pilgrimage ten miles from Havana. It is here, in the humble working-class town of San Francisco de Paula, that the legendary author wrote three of his most famous books: *For Whom the Bell Tolls, The Old Man and the Sea*, and a *Moveable Feast*. Hemingway's wife at the time, the journalist Martha Gellhorn, discovered the Spanish Colonial home, sprawled across fifteen acres, in 1939. Even after the couple divorced in 1945, Hemingway continued to reside there until a year after the Revolution in 1960, one year before he committed suicide. *Pilar*, the author's celebrated boat, is parked on the property, and three of his beloved cats are buried alongside it.

The house itself is a virtual museum, with priceless paintings from artists like Miró and Picasso in between the mounted heads of lions and antelope that the notorious wild game hunter shot dead in Africa. Everything remains just as it was when Hemingway sold the house, as if time stopped the moment he stepped out the door for the last time. The Cuban government claims that the house is in stellar shape, despite its being listed as one of

the eleven most endangered historical sites in the world. Though the debate as to its condition rages on between Cuba and the rest of the world, one aspect of Hemingway is unshakable: the Cuban people's adoration of him.

With our guide, Pepe, we enjoyed Hemingway's beverage of choice, a cocktail of sugarcane juice, rum, lime, and pineapple that is served on the grounds of the property. It comes in terra-cotta cups engraved with the logo of three arrowheads that Hemingway used to symbolize the property. We wondered why the author was still worshipped so many decades after he bid farewell to Cuba. Pepe explained in his wise, eloquent fashion: "Hemingway touched the soul of the Cuban people. When he won the Nobel Peace Prize he dedicated it to the Cubans. He represented to us the soul of the American people in such a beautiful light. He lived with grace, and we revere him. We existed with him in a mutual state of respect and solidarity. It is absolute. It is the same relationship that the Cuban people hope in their deepest hearts that we still have with the American people. We seek an unwavering fellowship even after all these years of separation. Hemingway is that idealized America for us. He is our Papa."

a cheat sheet for cuba's top ten cocktails

mojito

A refreshing libation of lime, rum, simple syrup, sparkling water, and muddled mint leaves typically served in a highball glass over ice.

caipirinha

This cocktail originated in Brazil, but Cubans have made it their own. It's made from a distilled sugarcane juice blended with lime and sugar and served over ice.

cubanito

A Cuban Bloody Mary blended with tomato juice, lime, Worcestershire sauce, sugar, salt, a dash of hot sauce, and of course, a generous splash of rum.

cuba libre

A rum and Coke with the addition of fresh lime served over ice.

havana special

A blend of white rum, maraschino cherry liqueur, and pineapple juice served over ice.

mary pickford

A twist on the Havana Special of white rum, maraschino cherry liqueur, and pineapple juice that's made even sweeter with the addition of grenadine syrup. It's named after the actress Mary Pickford, who took a trip to Cuba in the early twentieth century with Douglas Fairbanks and Charlie Chaplin.

daiquiri

An entire family of cocktails with endless variations; its foundation includes white rum, simple syrup, and lime syrup. It's served with blended ice and often contains fruit juice as a flavoring agent.

mulata

A rich blend of dark rum, dark and light crème de cacaos, freshly squeezed lime juice, and simple syrup.

saoco

A combination of rum and coconut water served over ice.

isla de pinos

A refreshing blend of grapefruit juice with a splash of white rum.

During our second visit to Cuba we were invited into a multiple-family home with a communal bathroom. The young son of one of the families took a liking to us and was intrigued by the camera lenses we were using. We started to show him the images we'd captured, and then he turned the situation around and started taking pictures of us instead. It's a memory we never tire of. His mother offered us a shot of homemade "rum," and although we were leery of it at first, our own mothers' reminder to be polite and graciously accept whatever is offered to you convinced us to toss the shot back. And then another. And another. We paid for it the next day, but that's not what left the most indelible impression. What really stuck with us was the way the patriarch of the family refused to eat until everyone else, including all of his neighbors, had been fed. This gesture embodies the generosity of the Cuban spirit for us, and although this recipe is called a Bitter Cuban, it's a character trait we would rarely associate with the friends we made there.

BITTER CUBAN

MAKES 1 SERVING

3 brandied cherries

½ teaspoon sugar

2 ounces rum

10 drops orange bitters

Ice

Strip of orange peel

Add the cherries and sugar to a cocktail shaker and lightly muddle with a spoon. Add the rum, bitters, and ice and give it a good shake. Pour into a rocks glass and garnish with the orange peel.

CAFÉ CUBANO

MAKES 3 SHOTS OR ⅓ CUP

Prepare the espresso in a six-serving stove-top espresso maker or French press. Pour the first draw of the espresso over the sugar (just enough to wet it). While the rest of the espresso is brewing, whip the sugar and espresso with a spoon or small whisk until it becomes foamy and lightens in color. Mix in the rest of the espresso, letting the foam rise. Pour into espresso cups and serve immediately.

Café Arcangel, right across the street from the paladar La Guarida (see page 37) and next door to our friend Reuben's home that he shares with his sister and brother-in-law, serves some of the finest roasted coffee in Havana. The lively space has red-painted walls graced with abstract watercolors and ink drawings. On Saturday nights it is transformed into a piano bar, but no matter what time of day it is, the owners never waver from their commitment to roasting Cuban beans to nutty perfection. As noted, with the export of nearly all of Cuba's coffee beans, there isn't a robust roasting culture in the nation. But times are changing, and as more and more Cubans get their hands on their own coffee beans, independent coffee shops will inevitably flourish. For now there is still a meager selection, but Café Arcangel makes up for that deficit with its finely roasted coffee and breezy, inviting atmosphere.

This recipe combines two of Cuba's most beloved ingredients, coffee and rum, in a cinnamon-spiked drink perfect to kick off a lazy summer afternoon.

CAFÉ CUBANO BATIDO

MAKES 1 SERVING

1 cup whole milk
½ cup Café Cubano (page 226)
¼ cup dulce de leche
1½ ounces dark rum (optional)
¾ cup crushed ice
Grated cinnamon, for garnish

Combine all of the ingredients except the cinnamon in a blender and blend until frothy. Garnish with grated cinnamon.

Batido, or *licuado* in other parts of the Caribbean, Mexico, and the Americas, roughly means "beaten," an appropriate moniker for what is essentially a Cuban smoothie. They are made to order throughout Havana and come in a dizzying array of combinations, from guava and mango to lime and tamarind spiked with chile. In this version, we've added oats to thicken it up a bit. Consider this a foundational recipe to get your creative smoothie juices flowing (pardon the pun).

OATMEAL MANGO BATIDO

MAKES 1 SERVING

½ cup thick rolled oats
1½ cups whole milk
½ cup fresh mango chunks
¼ cup sugar
1 cup crushed ice
Juice of 1 to 2 limes
Orange zest, for garnish

Combine all of the ingredients except the lime juice in a blender and blend until smooth. Blend in the lime juice a little at a time, to taste. Serve immediately.

ICED TEA
WITH MANGO-LIME PUREE

MAKES 1 SERVING

1 mango, peeled and diced

1 cup strong brewed black tea, chilled

Juice of 2 limes

1 tablespoon sugar

Ice

Mint leaves, for garnish

Fresh mango or lime slices, for garnish

Puree the mango in a blender. Add the chilled tea, lime juice, and sugar and blend until incorporated. Serve chilled or over ice. Garnish with mint leaves and mango or lime slices.

GUARAPO (SORT OF . . .)

MAKES 1 SERVING

2 ounces light rum

1 ounce cane sugar simple syrup

1 ounce freshly squeezed lime juice

Ice

Lime wedge, for garnish

Combine the rum, simple syrup, lime juice, and ice in a cocktail shaker. Shake well for at least 30 seconds. Strain and serve over ice, garnished with the lime wedge.

This cocktail is ideal for a sophisticated evening when only something extraordinary will do. Passion fruit is available in its pureed form in the frozen food section of many supermarkets, or better yet, if fresh passion fruit is available, prepare it on the spot.

PASSION FRUIT MARTINI

MAKES 1 SERVING

2 ounces light rum
1 ounce passion fruit puree
1 ounce simple syrup
2 dashes Peychaud's Bitters
Ice

Shake all the ingredients in a cocktail shaker for 20 to 30 seconds. Strain and serve in a martini glass.

The Taino word *daiquiri* is one of the few indigenous words remaining in the Cuban language. While its meaning is unknown, one thing is certain: this classic Cuban cocktail—invented by the American engineer Jennings Cox, who was working in the country during the Ten Years' War at the end of the nineteenth century—has always had an illustrious following. Even Ernest Hemingway and President John F. Kennedy were smitten, and we're sure you will be too after trying this version made from mango and strawberry purees. In also contains Velvet Falernum, a tropical simple syrup made with aromatics including ginger, cloves, almonds, and sometimes allspice and vanilla. It adds a nuanced flavor to this celebrated Cuban drink.

STRAWBERRY MANGO DAIQUIRI

MAKES 6 SERVINGS

1 cup fresh strawberry puree
1 cup fresh mango puree
2 ounces freshly squeezed lemon juice
1 ounce simple syrup
9 ounces light rum
3 ounces Velvet Falernum
Ice
6 lemon twists, for garnish

Blend the purees, lemon juice, and simple syrup ahead of time. When ready to serve, for each drink shake 3 ounces of this mix with 1½ ounces light rum and ½ ounce Velvet Falernum in a cocktail shaker with ice. Strain and serve in a martini glass with a lemon twist.

CUBA LIBRE

MAKES 1 SERVING

1½ ounces light rum
Juice of ½ lime
Ice
Coca-Cola
Lime wedge, for garnish

Add the rum and lime juice to a highball glass filled with ice. Top off with Coca-Cola and garnish with the lime wedge.

SPICED RUM PIMM'S CUP

MAKES 1 SERVING

4 cucumber slices

½ ounce freshly squeezed lime juice

2 ounces spiced rum

3 dashes Peychaud's Bitters

Ginger beer

Mint sprig, for garnish

Wide strip of orange zest, for garnish

Lightly muddle 2 of the cucumber slices in a highball glass. Add the lime juice, rum, and bitters. Top with ginger beer. Garnish with the remaining cucumber and the mint and orange zest.

What would Cuba be without the mojito? We shudder to think! This classic cocktail has murky origins, but it is clearly the drink of choice for many Cubans seeking to cool off on hot summer days. The drink is now ubiquitous in bars the world over, but it's best enjoyed in Cuba, bellying up to the bar at La Bodeguita del Medio, Ernest Hemingway's favorite pit stop for one of his preferred Cuban cocktails.

MOJITO

MAKES 1 SERVING

Half of a lime, quartered
8 to 10 mint leaves
½ ounce simple syrup
1½ ounces light rum
Soda water
Mint sprig, for garnish
Lime wedge, for garnish

Lightly muddle the quartered lime and mint leaves with the simple syrup in a highball glass. Add ice and rum and top with soda water. Garnish with the mint sprig and the lime wedge.

the cuban pantry

BIJOL

A commercial blend of ground achiote seed with the addition of coloring agents, cumin, and corn flour, used as a golden coloring agent in many Cuban dishes. It bestows the faintest hint of sweet chile on a dish, a flavor synonymous with many Cuban recipe classics. It is frequently used as a stand-in for dishes requiring saffron. In a pinch, turmeric can be used as a substitute.

CHORIZO

A classic Spanish pork sausage, traditionally spiced with smoked paprika but sometimes made with native red chiles in Cuba that not only spice up its flavor but also impart a deep red color. It is enjoyed cured and semi-cured throughout the nation and is sometimes used as a paste in dishes such as tostones or slathered on bread for a hearty afternoon snack.

CONCH

Cubans have a long tradition of incorporating conch into their recipes, much as cooks have done throughout the Caribbean for centuries. This meaty animal, producer and inhabitant of large sea shells (which deliver the sound of the ocean into our ears), is best when consumed unadulterated, freshly plucked from the ocean. It's also popular in Cuba in chowders, seviche, fritters, and salads.

FUFU

Smashed green plantains served alongside stews or other dishes with thick gravies.

HELADO

Ice cream, a beloved dessert in Cuba.

MALANGA

A starchy, high-calorie root vegetable that is frequently boiled and served as a side dish in Cuba.

MOJO

Hot spices are rarely used in Cuban cooking, and mojo sauce is the primary flavor delivery agent in many recipes. Its components vary, but at its most elemental it includes garlic, oregano, citrus juice, and oil.

PLANTAINS

A banana relative, starchy green plantains are served as a savory component of many meals. They're frequently fried to accompany congri, or black rice and beans.

SOFRITO

A secret ingredient in many Cuban dishes, sofrito is a combination of slowly cooked onions, bell pepper, and garlic. Tomatoes and/or cilantro are other common sofrito ingredients.

SUGARCANE

This subtropical grass that flourishes throughout Cuba is the nation's primary source of sugar and, let's not forget, rum.

TOSTONES

Green plantains that are sliced and fried, then pressed, and fried once more. They're served unadulterated in Cuba but also stuffed with delicacies like lobster, crab, or pork.

YUCA

Not to be confused with the ornamental yucca plant, this root vegetable of the evergreen family is related to malanga. The starchy white tuber is often boiled to a sweet, candy-like consistency. It's a ubiquitous and highly nutritious mainstay on the Cuban table.

acknowledgments

FROM DAN AND ANDREA

This book is dedicated to the Cuban people, their resilient spirit, delicious food, and beautiful culture. They welcomed us with open arms and showed us that it is not how much you have, but how much you enjoy life that truly makes you happy.

MOLLIE HAYWARD You transformed simple ingredients into delicious dishes. Your food styling and dedication are why these recipes came to life. Thanks so much for all of your hard work. We are so happy you were able to collaborate on this book with us, our Mojo Queen.

BETH MAY Thank you for your unique design work on this book and for your "out of the box" aesthetic. It has been a spectacular collaboration and your vision has taken the design of our book to another level.

NICOLE J. RUIZ Our very own Shirley Temple. You are a rock star producer and we could not have done this project without you. Your mad skills kept us organized, on time, well fed and most importantly heavily caffeinated. Your constant support, advice and sarcasm have not gone unnoticed. Thank you for always having a smile on your face. Your friendship and dedication is greatly appreciated.

BECKI SCHOLL To our fabulous mixologist. Thanks for taking our vision and making it better! Your creativity and devotion to your craft have turned classic Cuban cocktails into fun, modern drinks with a twist. Cheers!

JODY EDDY Thanks for hopping on a plane and meeting us in Cuba to take on this project with enthusiasm and eagerness. We appreciate you working countless late-nights to make these stories come to life. Your beautiful words have really given this book heart and a voice.

THE CREW Samer Almadani, thank you for your spectacular retouching, great attitude, and work ethic. Travas Machel, thanks for all the big and fluffies and all of your help on set. Erin Quon, who started this journey with us. Your culinary skills are only over shadowed by your great big heart and infectious spirit. Andy Rosenstein, for all of your help and for keeping Mollie smiling in the kitchen. Will Smith, for your fabulous food styling, creativity and storytelling. Emilie Zanger, your copyediting skills were a lifesaver. Samantha Hylla and Jamie Bayer, for your digital teching magic. Jon Scott and Robert Rutherford, for your color correcting, printing and proofing. Amaurie and Ruben, who took us places we may have never seen and for never saying no.

TEN SPEED PRESS Sincere thanks to the incredible team at Ten Speed Press. Jenny Wapner, for believing in us and allowing us to realize our dream. Kara Plikaitis, for your beautiful sense of design, art direction and patience. We owe you a gin and tonic! Hannah Rahill, for giving us the opportunity and taking a risk. Emma Campion, for making this book as functional as it is beautiful. Clara Sankey, for making sure we never missed our deadlines and keeping us on our toes. It does take a village, and we needed the whole team's guidance to make this book happen. We are so grateful you took a chance on us. Thank you for everything!

FROM DAN

MY WIFE & DAUGHTER Casey and Dylan, thank you for holding down the fort when I am traveling, and thank you for putting up with me when I'm tired and "hangry". You have always inspired me to follow my dreams and I am very thankful. This book has been a long journey and you have been there for me every step of the way.

FAMILY Mom and Dad, thank you for encouraging me to go to art school and to follow my dreams. I appreciate your love and support.

ANDREA KUHN Thank you for pushing me to always do better! For making this book the best it could possibly be. Your brilliant creativity, unique styling and indistinguishable aesthetic are what make this book so engaging. Your dedication, hard work, and hysterical sense of humor are what got me through the long hours on this project.

TERRY HEFFERNAN Thank you for being my mentor and teaching me your craft. You have taught me so much and your passion continues to influence me.

EMISSARY ARTISTS Thank you Liz and Stacey, for keeping my business going while I'm traveling in Cuba. You both help to guide me forward in my career, sometimes with a nudge and sometimes with a push! Your friendship and advice mean so much to me.

FROM ANDREA

MY MOTHER Lillian Kuhn, who always encouraged me to follow my passion and always believed in me.

MY BROTHERS AND SISTER Jeffrey, Stuffy, Arnie, and Tari for putting up with their baby sister all these years and always taking good care of me. Thankfully, I was able to pay you back for that grilled cheese sandwich.

MY FAMILY AND FRIENDS For all of their support and constant enthusiasm for my Cuban adventures.

DAN GOLDBERG What can I say? You are the best partner in crime. Thank you for supporting all of my crazy ideas. Your dedication, perseverance and amazing photography are what drives this book, and made my work look that much better. You made me laugh through this whole process, sometimes at your expense. I will always treasure my memories of "lifelong friends" and jokey drinks. Thank you for letting me ride shotgun on this crazy, wild adventure.

LUCY & FINLEY Lastly, I'd like to thank Lucy and Finley, our mascots and the best dogs a girl can ask for. They kept the studio smiling and our blood pressures down. Lucy started this crazy journey with us and Finley has taken over in her path fearlessly. They truly are a girl's best friend.

FROM JODY

I would like to thank my mother, Mary Eddy, who placed such significance on traveling to new places and my grandmother, Evelyn Bragelman, who reminded me to always return to the shore where she waited. I would also like to thank my agent, Amy Collins and my editor, Jenny Wapner, who believed in this project from the very beginning. I would also like to thank the extraordinary Cuban people for their generosity, optimism, graciousness, and unrivaled hospitality.

INDEX

Cada dia hay que perfecionar
lo que hicimos ayer

Ché

Published in the United States by Ten Speed Press,
an imprint of the Crown Publishing Group, a division
of Penguin Random House LLC, New York.
www.crownpublishing.com
www.tenspeed.com

Ten Speed Press and the Ten Speed Press colophon
are registered trademarks of Penguin Random House LLC.

Library of Congress Cataloging-in-Publication
Data is on file with the publisher.

Hardcover ISBN: 978-1-60774-986-8
eBook ISBN: 978-1-60774-987-5

Printed in China

Design by Beth May
Production design by Kara Plikaitis
Recipe development by Mollie Hayward

10 9 8 7 6 5 4 3 2 1

First Edition